MIND WORKS

Thunder Bay Press

An imprint of Printers Row Publishing Group

10350 Barnes Canyon Road, Suite 100, San Diego, CA 92121

www.thunderbaybooks.com

Publisher: Peter Norton
Associate Publisher: Ana Parker
Publishing/Editorial Team: April Farr, Kelly Larsen, Kathryn C. Dalby
Editorial Team: JoAnn Padgett, Melinda Allman, Dan Mansfield

ISBN: 978-1-68412-934-8

All images: © iStockphoto & Shutterstock

Printed in Dubai

23 22 21 20 19   1 2 3 4 5

MIND WORKS

Ten IQ tests from the
masters of intelligence

Dr. Gareth Moore and Graham Jones

THUNDER BAY
P · R · E · S · S

San Diego, California

CONTENTS

INTRODUCTION

INTRODUCTION

Welcome to *Mind Works*! This colorful book is packed from cover to cover with a series of 10 comprehensive tests, each featuring 40 logic and number puzzles.

Your brain loves to learn, so alongside a handful of familiar puzzles I've also included a wide range of more unusual challenges. As a result, you will find a huge variety of material to both test and entertain you as you work your way through.

Some of the puzzles might take a bit of practice to get the hang of, but try not to skip over the ones that you find tricky – these are probably the ones that you will bring you most mental benefit. Your brain thrives on new challenges, and the more novel and unusual a task is, the better! If there are any puzzles where the rules aren't clear, there's nothing wrong with checking one of the solutions at the back to see how the puzzle works. You can use this to work out how the given clues connect with the resulting solution, which can be helpful for some of the more complex puzzles.

If you are struggling to get started on a puzzle, don't be afraid to make an intelligent guess. For some puzzle types, this may even be the quickest way to learn. Your brain is great at spotting patterns, so jump in and try something and see what happens – even if it doesn't work out, you'll still discover things about how the puzzle works, helping you to make your next guess even smarter.

The puzzles do become progressively harder as you proceed, so it's best to start at the beginning of the book and work your way through. It's also a good idea to complete an entire test, if you can, before moving onto the next, to help ensure you get the most comprehensive mind workout. Some of the puzzles within a test share some related concepts, too, so improving on one puzzle type may also help you with another.

The puzzles are all presented from a 3D perspective, adding some challenging visual reasoning elements to the puzzles. One effect of this dramatic presentation is that any references to "horizontal" or "vertical" in the instructions should be taken with regard to the angle the puzzle is drawn at, so if it is slanting down to the right then any "horizontal" lines will slant down to the right too. This might sound confusing, but all will become clear when you look at the relevant puzzles. A similar effect applies to any references to "rows" and "columns" too, where they will also follow the 3D perspective of the puzzle.

Finally, while your brain does indeed love novelty it's important to also note that it doesn't learn well when frustrated. If you get truly stuck on a puzzle, therefore, then don't be afraid to take a look at the solutions to "borrow" a few extra clues to get you going again. It's better to complete the puzzle with help than to abandon it entirely!

Most of all, remember to have fun!

Dr. Gareth Moore
London

THE TESTS

Test 1

01

Place a digit from 1 to 5 into every square, so that no digit repeats in any row or column. Numbers separated by a greater than or less than sign must obey that sign. Arrows always point to the smaller number of a pair.

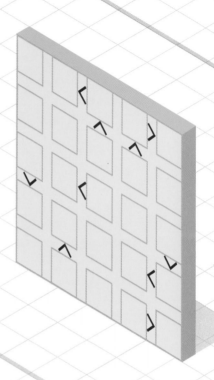

Answer see page 251

02

Draw paths to join pairs of matching coloured shapes. Paths can only travel in straight lines between the centres of squares, and no more than one path can enter any square. Paths cannot touch or cross.

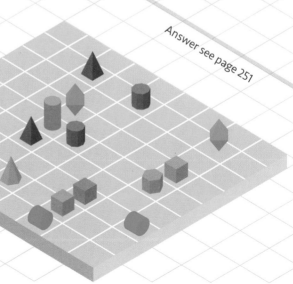

Answer see page 251

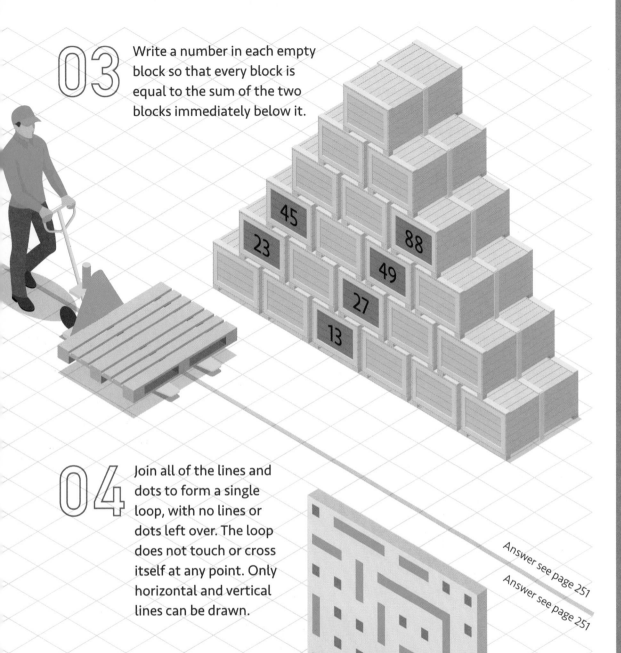

03 Write a number in each empty block so that every block is equal to the sum of the two blocks immediately below it.

04 Join all of the lines and dots to form a single loop, with no lines or dots left over. The loop does not touch or cross itself at any point. Only horizontal and vertical lines can be drawn.

Answer see page 251

Answer see page 251

05

Place a number from 1 to 6 once each into every row and column of the grid, while obeying the region clues. The value at the top left of each bold-lined region must be obtained when all of the numbers in that region have the given operation (+, −, ×, ÷) applied between them. For − and ÷ operations, begin with the largest number in the region and then subtract or divide by the other numbers in the region in any order.

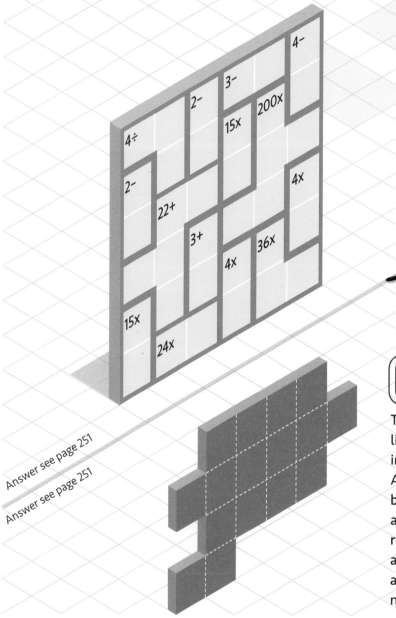

Answer see page 251

Answer see page 251

06

Trace along the dashed lines to divide up the area into four separate pieces. All of the pieces must be identical in shape, although they may be rotated relative to one another. Reflections that are not also rotations are not counted as identical.

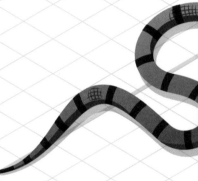

07

Place a colour into each empty square so that every colour appears once in each row, column and bold-lined jigsaw shape.

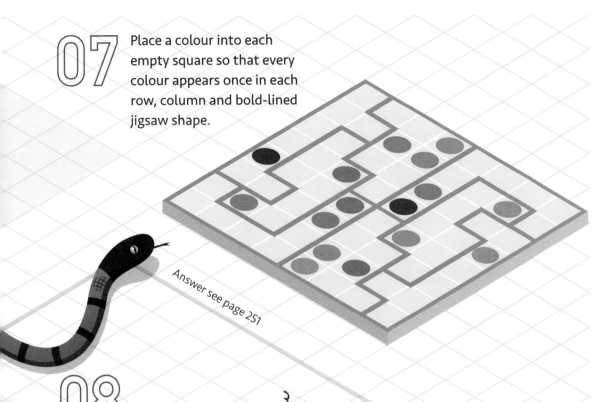

Answer see page 251

08

Shade some squares to form a snake that starts and ends at the snake eyes. Numbers outside the grid specify the number of squares in their row or column that contain part of the snake. A snake is a single path of adjacent shaded squares that does not branch. Shaded squares cannot touch, except for the immediately preceding and following squares in the snake. Shaded squares also cannot touch diagonally, except as necessary for the snake to turn a corner.

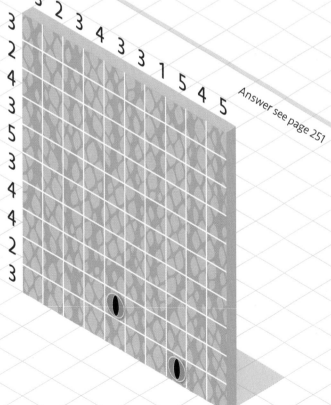

Answer see page 251

09

Place a digit from 1 to 5 into every square, so that no digit repeats in any row or column inside the grid. Place digits in such a way that each given clue number outside the grid represents the number of digits that are "visible" from that point, looking along that clue's row or column. A digit is visible if there is no higher digit preceding it.

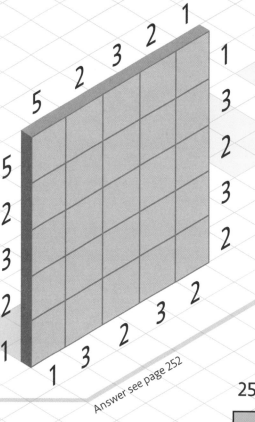

Answer see page 251

Answer see page 252

10

Place a number from 1 to 6 once each in every row and column. Values outside the grid give the total of the numbers in each of the indicated diagonals.

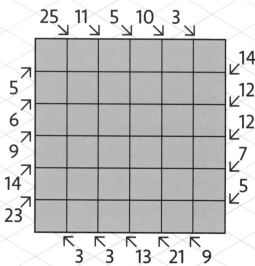

11 Draw along the dashed lines to divide the grid to form a complete set of standard dominoes, with exactly one of each domino. A "0" represents a blank on a traditional domino. Use the check-off chart (right) to help you keep track of which dominoes you've placed.

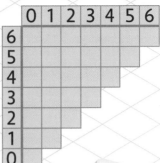

	0	1	2	3	4	5	6
6							
5							
4							
3							
2							
1							
0							

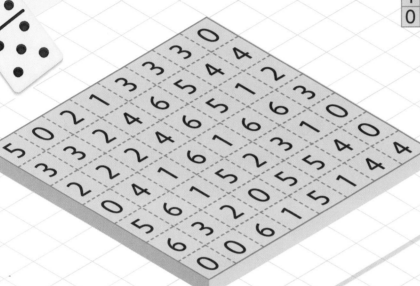

Grid values:
5 0 3 3 0
3 1 3 5 4 4 1 2
2 4 6 5 1 2 6 3
3 2 2 4 6 1 6 6 3 0
2 2 4 1 6 2 3 1 0 0
0 4 1 5 2 0 5 5 4
5 6 1 5 2 5 1 4 4
6 3 0 6
0 0 6

Answer see page 252

Answer see page 252

12 Place a letter from A to F into every square, so that no letter repeats in any row or column. Identical letters cannot be in diagonally touching squares.

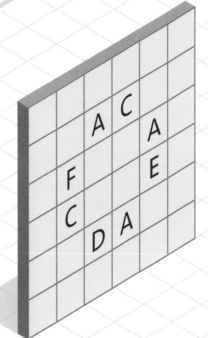

Grid clues:
A C
F E
A
C
D A

13 Draw a single loop by joining some dots so that each numbered square has the specified number of adjacent line segments. Dots can only be joined by horizontal or vertical lines, and the loop cannot touch, cross or overlap itself in any way.

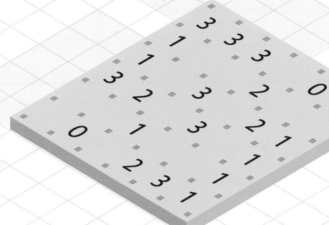

Answer see page 252

Answer see page 252

14 Place numbers from 1 to 9 so that each row, column and bold-lined 3x3 box contains one of each number. Numbers from 1 to 3 must be placed in regular grid squares; numbers from 4 to 6 must be placed in grid squares that contain a green circle; and numbers from 7 to 9 must be placed in grid squares that contain an orange circle.

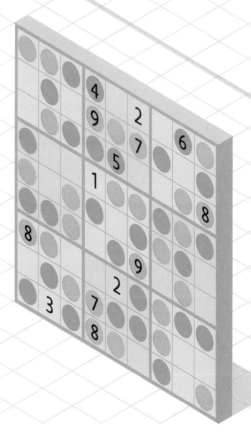

15 Join dots with horizontal and vertical lines to form a single path which does not touch or cross itself at any point. The start and end of the path are given by the red circles. Numbers outside the grid specify the number of dots in their row or column that are visited by the path.

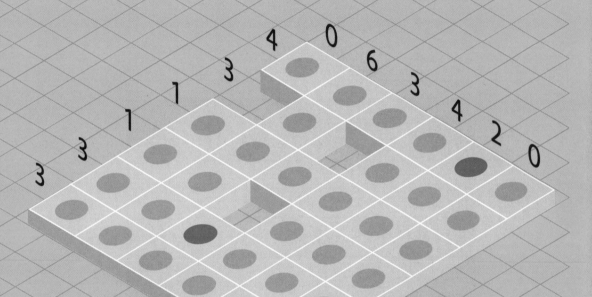

16

Place a digit from 1 to 9 into each yellow square, so that no digit repeats in any consecutive horizontal or vertical run of squares. Each horizontal or vertical run has a total given immediately to its left or above, respectively. The digits in that run must add up to the given total.

Answer see page 252

17 Reveal a hidden picture by shading some squares, while obeying the clues at the start of each row or column. The clues provide, in reading order, the length of every run of consecutive shaded squares in each row and column. There must be a gap of at least one empty square between each run of shaded squares in the same row or column.

	1	7	2	2 2	1 2 3	2 3	2 2	2 2	2	7
2										
5										
2, 2										
2, 2										
1, 2, 2, 1										
1, 2, 2, 1										
1, 1										
1, 2, 1										
1, 2, 1										
2, 2, 1										

Answer see page 252

18 Place a digit from 1 to 8 into every square, so that each digit appears once in every row and column. Squares separated by a pink peg must contain two consecutive numbers, such as 2 and 3. Squares separated by a red peg must contain numbers where one is twice the value of the other, such as 2 and 4. All possible dots are given, so if there is no dot, then a neighbouring pair can be neither consecutive nor have one be twice the value of the other. Where 1 and 2 are neighbours, either a red peg or a pink peg might be given, but not both.

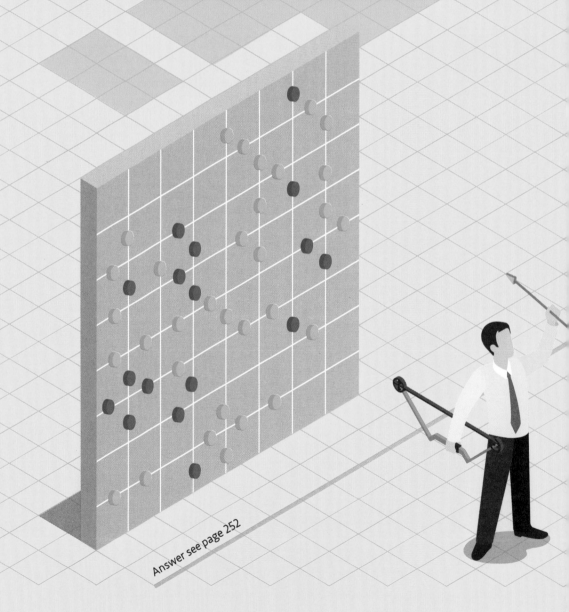

Answer see page 252

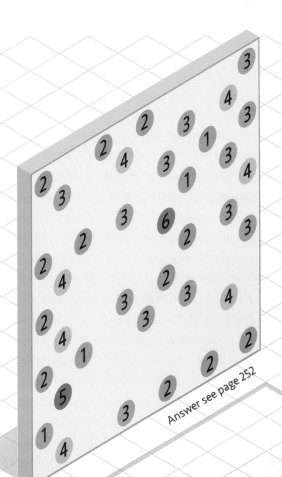

19

Draw horizontal and vertical lines along each row and column of circles to join circled numbers. Each circle contains a number which specifies the number of lines that connect to it. No more than two lines may join any pair of circles. Lines may not cross other lines or circles. All circles must be joined in such a way that you can travel from any circle to any other circle by following one or more lines.

Answer see page 252

20

Can you make each of the totals shown? For each total, choose one number from the outer ring, one number from the middle ring, and one number from the inner ring. The three numbers must add up to the given total.

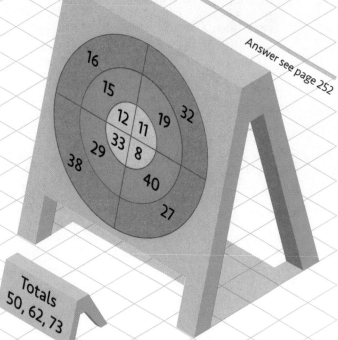

Answer see page 252

Totals
50, 62, 73

21

Write a number in each empty block so that every block is equal to the sum of the two blocks immediately below it.

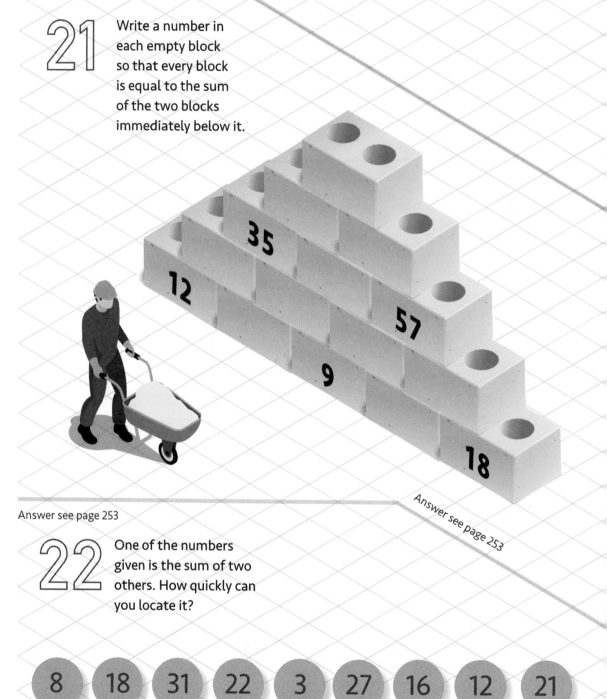

Answer see page 253

Answer see page 253

22

One of the numbers given is the sum of two others. How quickly can you locate it?

8   18   31   22   3   27   16   12   21

23 Fill the grid so that each row and column contains the colours red, green and blue, and two empty squares. The coloured digits surrounding the grid indicate which colour is encountered in which positions along that row or column. For example, a green 1 means the first colour encountered moving from the edge of the grid along the row or column is green, while a blue 2 means the second colour encountered is blue.

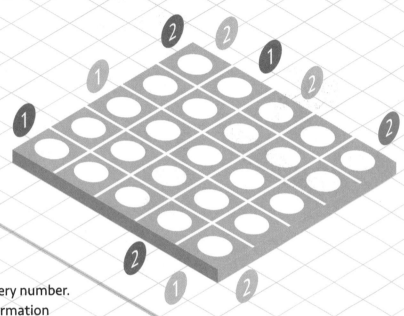

24

Identify the mystery number. Compare the information beside the given numbers. Each digit that appears in the mystery number is marked by a dot. Green indicates a digit in the correct position, red if not. Here, 5892 shares two digits with the mystery number, but only one digit is in the correct position.

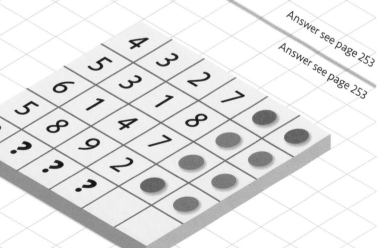

Answer see page 253

Answer see page 253

25 Three of the four animals pictured are odd in relation to the other three. Which of the four is a perfect match with the other three?

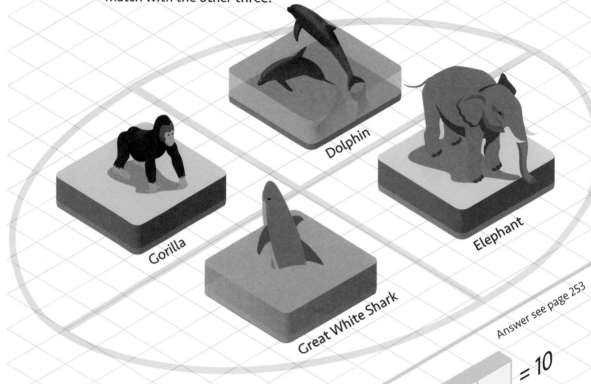

Dolphin

Gorilla

Great White Shark

Elephant

Answer see page 253

Answer see page 253

26 Fill the grid with the digits 1-9 to make the sums work. Solve from left to right and top to bottom in sequence – rules regarding the order of mathematical operations do not apply.

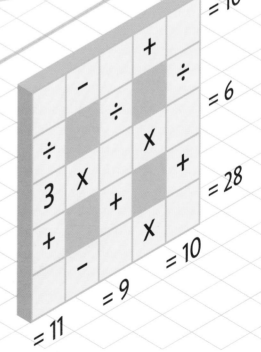

27 What number completes the sequence?

6   15   35   77   143   ?

Answer see page 253

Answer see page 253

28

Fit the listed numbers into the grid.

3 digits			4 digits	5 digits	
123	432	692	3274	31122	64344
194	495	725	3275	34972	69458
343	549	754		37165	71492
365	567	827		47365	
389	685			53285	

29

Fill in the blank shape following the below rules:

The green hexagon is the only hexagon that hasn't moved. It is still touching two of the same colours. The orange hexagon has moved to an adjacent position around the border, and the purple hexagon has moved two spaces. The orange and purple hexagons are adjacent, as are pink and orange. Neither pink nor yellow are touching blue.

Answer see page 253

30

What is the value represented by the question mark?

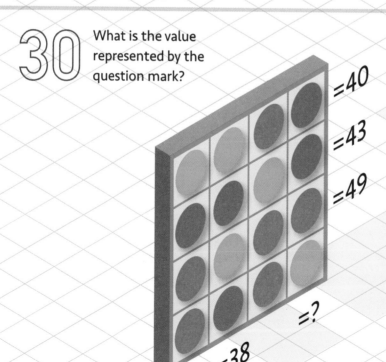

$=40$

$=43$

$=49$

$=38$

$=?$

Answer see page 253

3 1 The first two scales shown are balanced. How many cubes are needed to balance the third?

1

2

3

Answer see page 253

32

Three groundbreaking astronauts are touring the country with a show about their experiences. From the information below, work out how long each astronaut was in space, at which space station, and their favourite space activity.

Commander Cork spent 19 months away from his family, which was longer in space than Sergeant Starr, whose favourite space activity wasn't the space walk. The science experiments weren't the activity of choice for Captain Picky, who spent his time at Space Station Urania; he wasn't the astronaut who spent the least time – 16 months – in space. Space Station Selena was a home from home for the astronaut who enjoyed filter cleaning. Space Station Venus did not host the astronaut who spent 21 months in orbit.

Answer see page 254

33

We've given you two separate equations. Each uses the same digits and each of the mathematical operations +, –, x and ÷. Use each of the given numbers to complete each equation. Solve in sequence from left to right – rules regarding the order of mathematical operations do not apply.

Answer see page 254

3 5 6 9 12

$$\bigcirc \div \bigcirc + \bigcirc - \bigcirc \times \bigcirc = 60$$

$$\bigcirc - \bigcirc \times \bigcirc \div \bigcirc + \bigcirc = 7$$

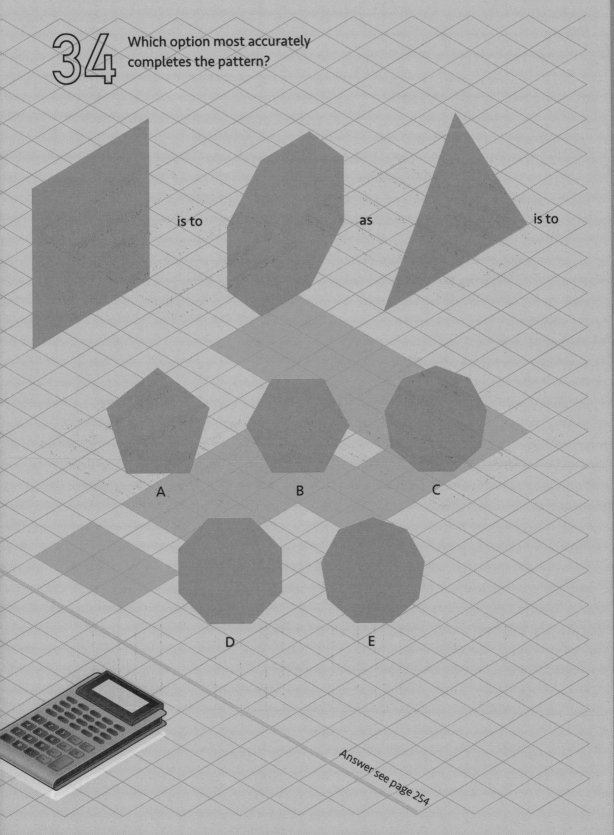

34

Which option most accurately completes the pattern?

is to

as

is to

A

B

C

D

E

Answer see page 254

35

The four images follow a pattern. Which option continues the sequence?

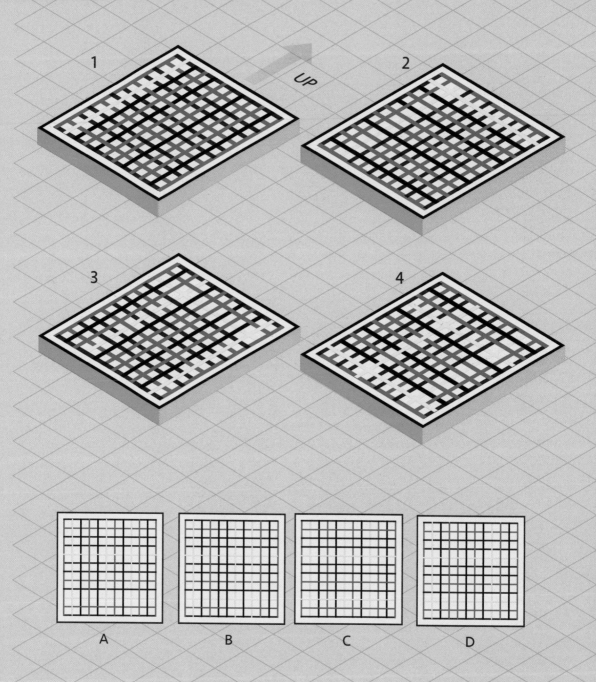

UP

1

2

3

4

A

B

C

D

Answer see page 254

36

Each set of numbers represents the name of a female singer, the letters of which have been encoded according to the telephone number pad shown. Who are the singers?

2 3 3 5 3
2 4 3 7
6 2 3 6 6 6 2
7 4 4 2 6 6 2
7 4 2 5 4 7 2
2 3 9 6 6 2 3

Answer see page 254

Answer see page 254

37

Fill the 3x3 grid with each of the listed colours as directed: red, orange, yellow, green, blue, purple, pink, brown, black. All references refer to the same row or column, so that "A is above B" means A and B are in the same column, while "C is to the right/left of D" means C and D are in the same row. Yellow is above black, which is to the right of blue. Brown, above both green and purple, is to the left of pink. Red is above blue and to the right of purple. Pink is above blue and to the left of yellow.

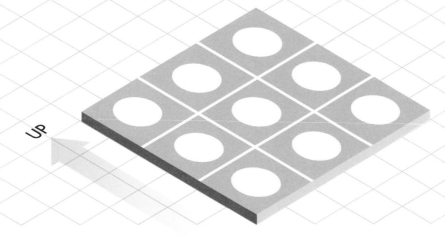

38

All the answers in this "crossword" are numbers. The unclued answer is a date (month, day, year) of significance in education.

1	2		3		4	
5					6	7
	8	9		10		
11						
12	13		14		15	
16					17	18
	19					

Across

1 1 Down reversed x first two digits of 7 Down x 161

5 $4^2 + 5^2$

6 4^3

8 UNCLUED

12 19 Across – 1 Across

16 5 Across + 17 Across

17 Last two digits of 14 Down

19 Product of the three highest prime numbers below 100

Down

1 $3^2 + 5^2$

2 4 Down + 51

3 7 Down – 11 Down

4 10 x 17 Across

7 1 Down x 5 Across reversed

9 Reverse of 14 Down + 50

10 11 Down x 7

11 Last three digits of 19 Across multiplied together

13 3 Down + 4 Down + 7 Down

14 29×2^2

15 13,008 ÷ 17 Across

18 1 Down + last two digits of 11 Down

Answer see page 254

39

(Legs on a woodlouse x rings on the Olympic flag) − (Atomic number of oxygen + holes on a regulation golf course)

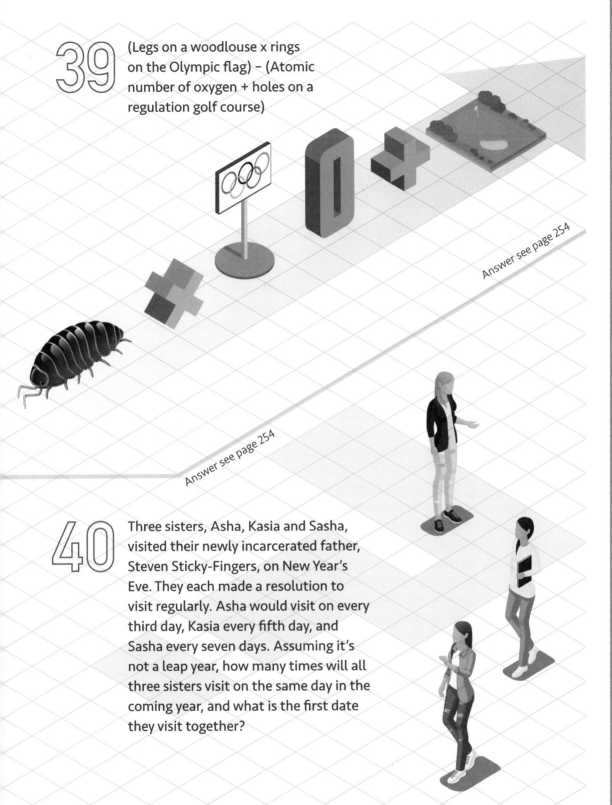

Answer see page 254

40

Three sisters, Asha, Kasia and Sasha, visited their newly incarcerated father, Steven Sticky-Fingers, on New Year's Eve. They each made a resolution to visit regularly. Asha would visit on every third day, Kasia every fifth day, and Sasha every seven days. Assuming it's not a leap year, how many times will all three sisters visit on the same day in the coming year, and what is the first date they visit together?

Answer see page 254

Test 2

01

Place a digit from 1 to 5 into every square, so that no digit repeats in any row or column. Numbers separated by a greater than or less than sign must obey that sign. Arrows always point to the smaller number of a pair.

Answer see page 254

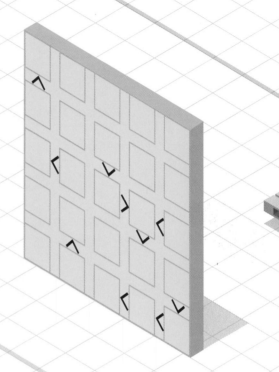

02

Draw paths to join pairs of matching coloured shapes. Paths can only travel in straight lines between the centres of squares, and no more than one path can enter any square. Paths cannot touch or cross.

Answer see page 254

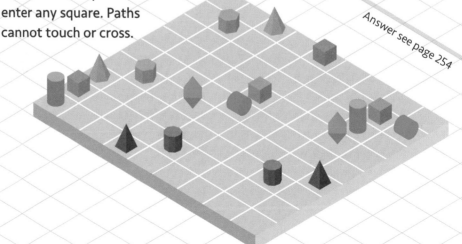

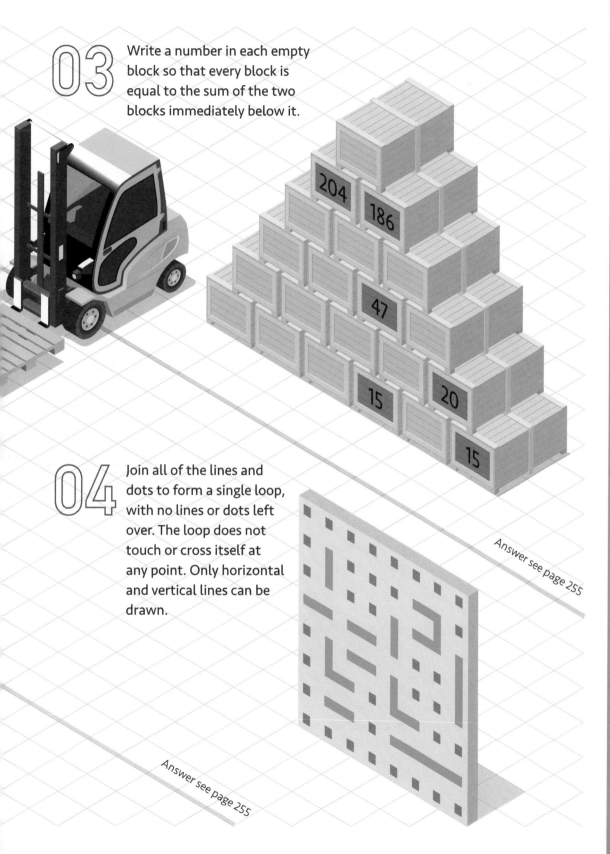

03

Write a number in each empty block so that every block is equal to the sum of the two blocks immediately below it.

204 186

47

15 20

15

Answer see page 255

04

Join all of the lines and dots to form a single loop, with no lines or dots left over. The loop does not touch or cross itself at any point. Only horizontal and vertical lines can be drawn.

Answer see page 255

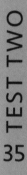

Place a number from 1 to 6 once each into every row and column of the grid, while obeying the region clues. The value at the top left of each bold-lined region must be obtained when all of the numbers in that region have the given operation (+, −, ×, ÷) applied between them. For − and ÷ operations, begin with the largest number in the region and then subtract or divide by the other numbers in the region in any order.

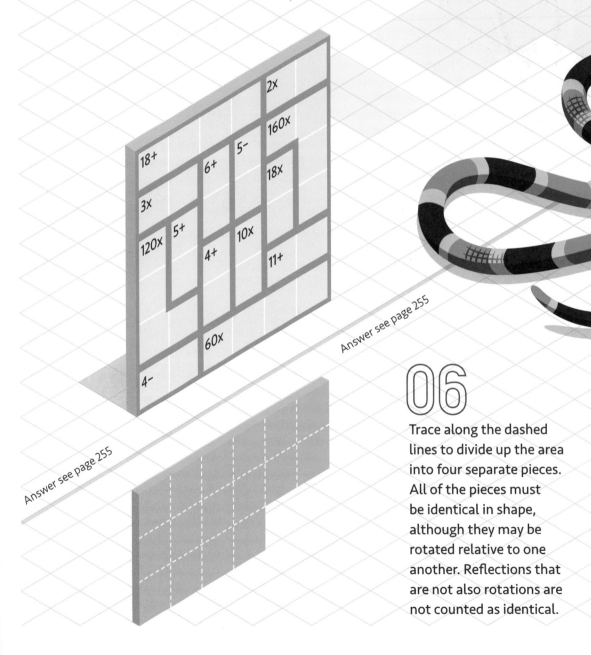

Answer see page 255

Answer see page 255

Trace along the dashed lines to divide up the area into four separate pieces. All of the pieces must be identical in shape, although they may be rotated relative to one another. Reflections that are not also rotations are not counted as identical.

07

Place a colour into each empty square so that every colour appears once in each row, column and bold-lined jigsaw shape.

Answer see page 255

08

Shade some squares to form a snake that starts and ends at the snake eyes. Numbers outside the grid specify the number of squares in their row or column that contain part of the snake. A snake is a single path of adjacent shaded squares that does not branch. Shaded squares cannot touch, except for the immediately preceding and following squares in the snake. Shaded squares also cannot touch diagonally, except as necessary for the snake to turn a corner.

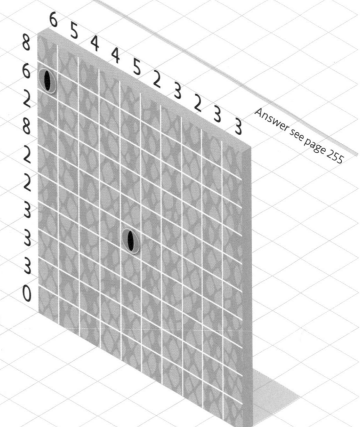

Answer see page 255

09

Place a digit from 1 to 5 into every square, so that no digit repeats in any row or column inside the grid. Place digits in such a way that each given clue number outside the grid represents the number of digits that are "visible" from that point, looking along that clue's row or column. A digit is visible if there is no higher digit preceding it.

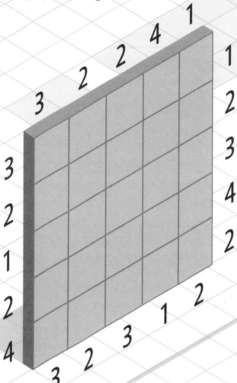

Answer see page 255
Answer see page 255

10

Place a number from 1 to 6 once each in every row and column. Values outside the grid give the total of the numbers in each of the indicated diagonals.

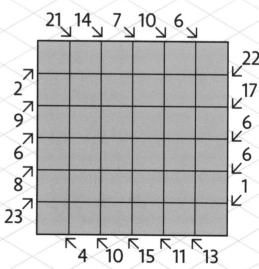

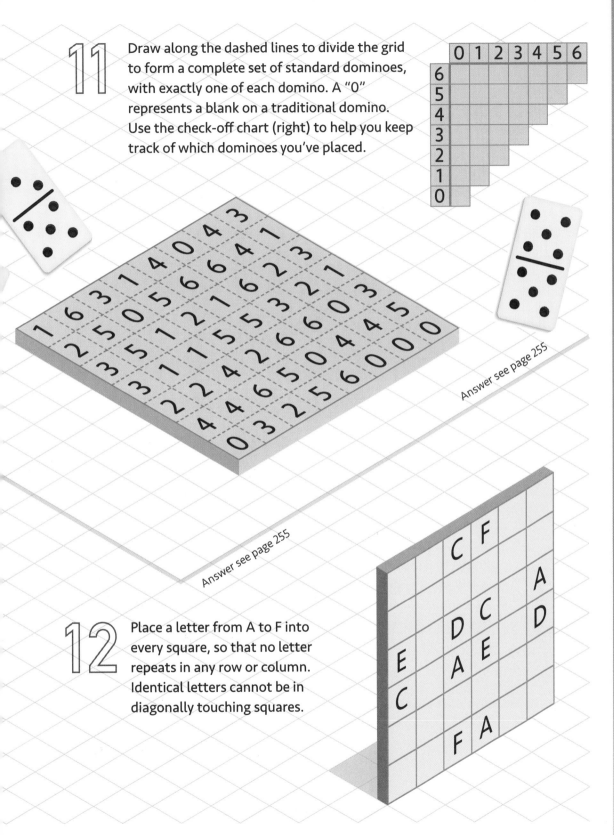

11 Draw along the dashed lines to divide the grid to form a complete set of standard dominoes, with exactly one of each domino. A "0" represents a blank on a traditional domino. Use the check-off chart (right) to help you keep track of which dominoes you've placed.

	0	1	2	3	4	5	6
6							
5							
4							
3							
2							
1							
0							

Grid numbers:
3 0 4 0 4 6 1
1 4 0 6 6 4 3 2
6 3 5 0 5 6 1 2 3
1 5 2 1 5 3 2 1 0
2 5 0 1 1 5 5 3 6 0 4 5
3 5 1 5 2 4 6 6 0 4 4 0 0
3 1 2 4 6 5 0 0
2 2 4 5 0 2 6
4 4 6 3 5 6
4 0 3 2

Answer see page 255

12 Place a letter from A to F into every square, so that no letter repeats in any row or column. Identical letters cannot be in diagonally touching squares.

Grid letters:
C F
D C A
E A E D
C
F A

Answer see page 255

13 Draw a single loop by joining some dots so that each numbered square has the specified number of adjacent line segments. Dots can only be joined by horizontal or vertical lines, and the loop cannot touch, cross or overlap itself in any way.

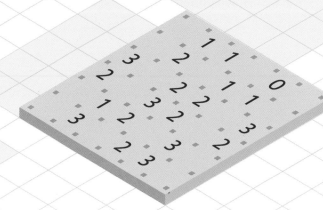

Answer see page 255

Answer see page 256

14 Place numbers from 1 to 9 so that each row, column and bold-lined 3x3 box contains one of each number. Numbers from 1 to 3 must be placed in regular grid squares; numbers from 4 to 6 must be placed in grid squares that contain a green circle; and numbers from 7 to 9 must be placed in grid squares that contain an orange circle.

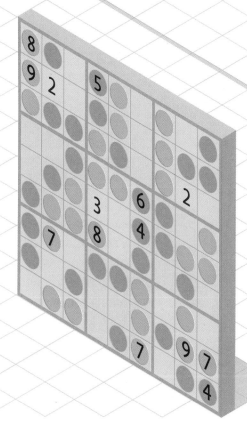

15 Join dots with horizontal and vertical lines to form a single path which does not touch or cross itself at any point. The start and end of the path are given by the red circles. Numbers outside the grid specify the number of dots in their row or column that are visited by the path.

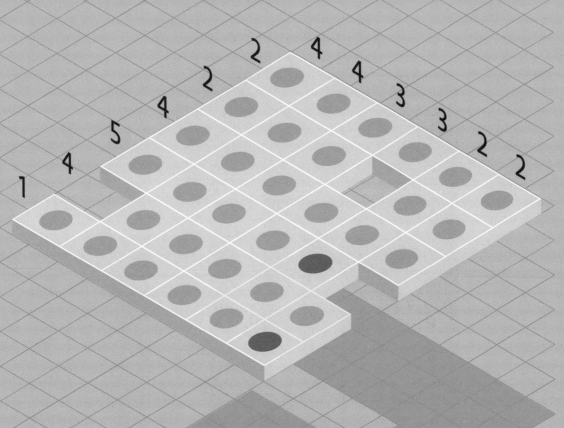

Answer see page 256

16 Place a digit from 1 to 9 into each yellow square, so that no digit repeats in any consecutive horizontal or vertical run of squares. Each horizontal or vertical run has a total given immediately to its left or above, respectively. The digits in that run must add up to the given total.

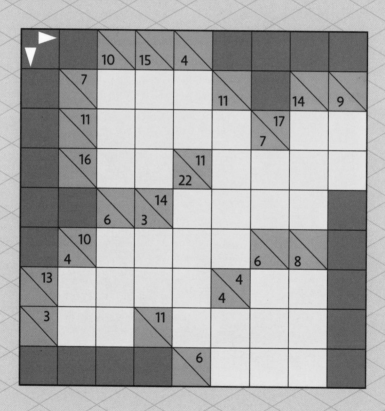

Answer see page 256

17 Reveal a hidden picture by shading some squares, while obeying the clues at the start of each row or column. The clues provide, in reading order, the length of every run of consecutive shaded squares in each row and column. There must be a gap of at least one empty square between each run of shaded squares in the same row or column.

	5	2 2	1 2	2 2	2 2	2 2	2 2	1 2	2 2	5
3, 3										
2, 4, 2										
1, 2, 1										
1, 1										
1, 1										
2, 2										
2, 2										
2, 2										
4										
2										

Answer see page 256

18

Place a digit from 1 to 8 into every square, so that each digit appears once in every row and column. Squares separated by a pink peg must contain two consecutive numbers, such as 2 and 3. Squares separated by a red peg must contain numbers where one is twice the value of the other, such as 2 and 4. All possible dots are given, so if there is no dot, then a neighbouring pair can be neither consecutive nor have one be twice the value of the other. Where 1 and 2 are neighbours, either a red peg or a pink peg might be given, but not both.

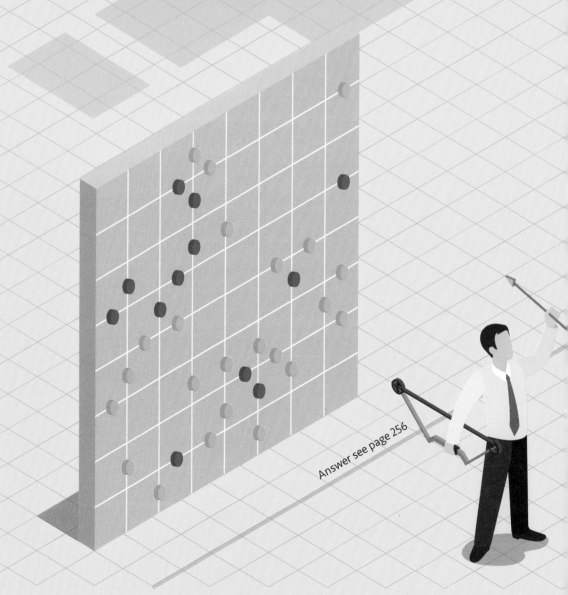

Answer see page 256

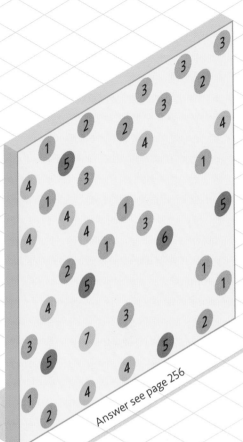

19 Draw horizontal and vertical lines along each row and column of circles to join circled numbers. Each circle contains a number which specifies the number of lines that connect to it. No more than two lines may join any pair of circles. Lines may not cross other lines or circles. All circles must be joined in such a way that you can travel from any circle to any other circle by following one or more lines.

Answer see page 256

Answer see page 256

20

Can you make each of the totals shown? For each total, choose one number from the outer ring, one number from the middle ring, and one number from the inner ring. The three numbers must add to the given total.

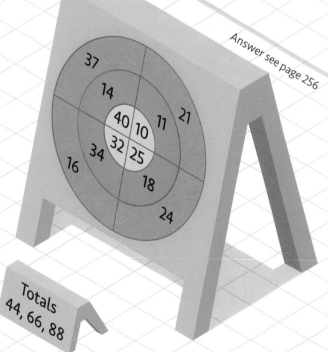

Totals
44, 66, 88

21 Write a number in each empty block so that every block is equal to the sum of the two blocks immediately below it.

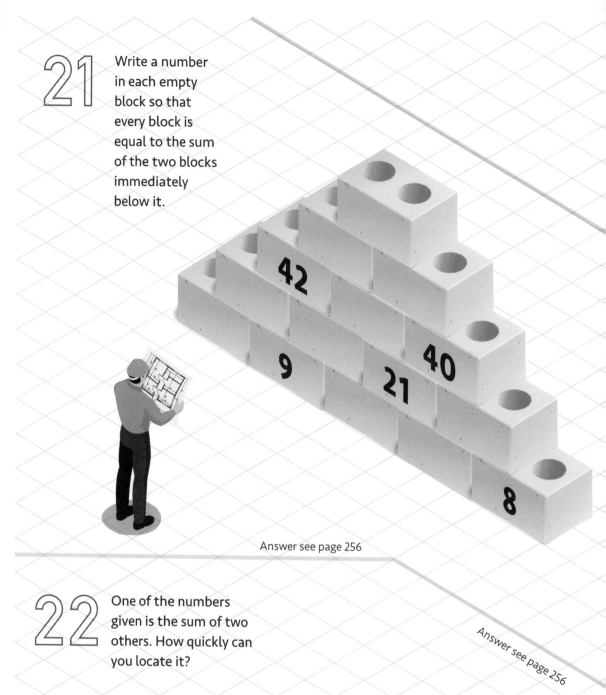

42

9   21   40

8

Answer see page 256

22 One of the numbers given is the sum of two others. How quickly can you locate it?

Answer see page 256

23   16   33   9   12   28   38   27   20

23 Fill the grid so that each row and column contains the colours red, green and blue, and two empty squares. The coloured digits surrounding the grid indicate which colour is encountered in which positions along that row or column. For example, a green 1 means the first colour encountered moving from the edge of the grid along the row or column is green, while a blue 2 means the second colour encountered is blue.

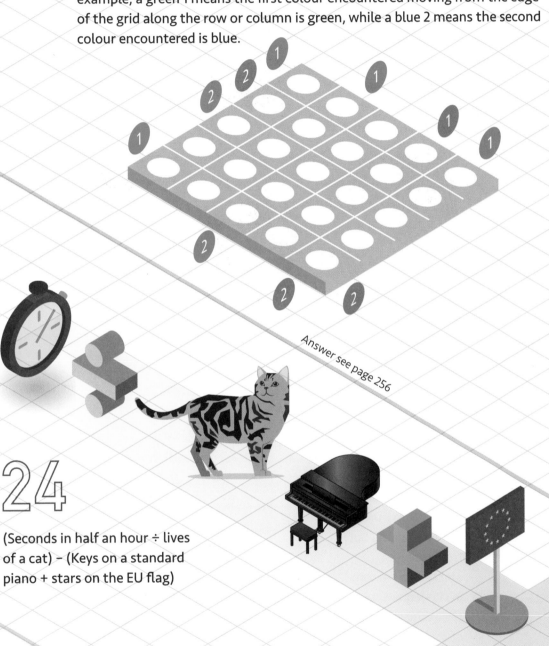

Answer see page 256

24

(Seconds in half an hour ÷ lives of a cat) – (Keys on a standard piano + stars on the EU flag)

Answer see page 256

25

Three of the four cities pictured are odd in relation to the other three. Which of the four is a perfect match with the other three?

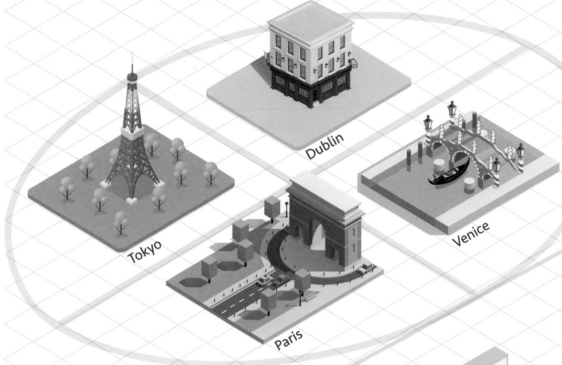

Dublin

Tokyo

Venice

Paris

Answer see page 257

Answer see page 257

26

Fill the grid with the digits 1-9 to make the sums work. Solve from left to right and top to bottom in sequence – rules regarding the order of mathematical operations do not apply.

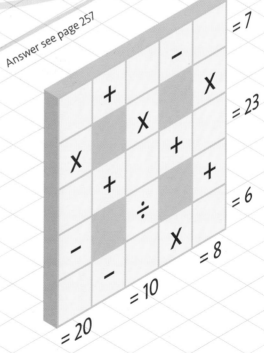

= 7

= 23

= 6

= 8

= 10

= 20

What number completes
the sequence?

Answer see page 257

Answer see page 257

1   1   3   15   105   ?

Fit the listed numbers
into the grid.

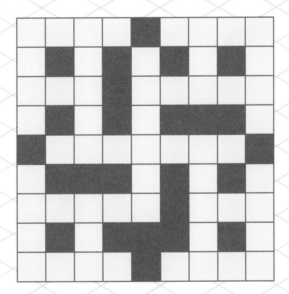

3 digits	4 digits		5 digits	6 digits
432	1739	4929	28672	624783
454	1845	6826	28688	
636	1946		31482	7 digits
846	3636		61483	5237829
	3824			
	4655			

29 Fill in the blank shape following the below rules:

The purple lozenge is the only one that hasn't moved. The blue lozenge is the only lozenge to have moved more than one space. It is adjacent to both the red and green lozenges.

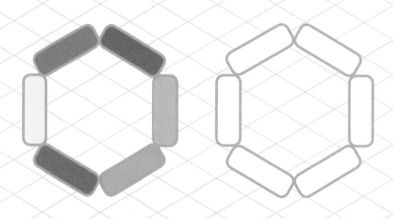

Answer see page 257

30 What is the value represented by the question mark?

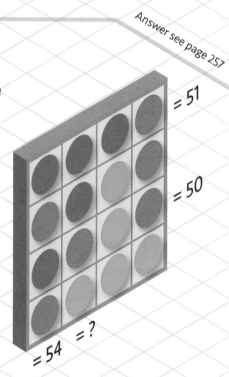

= 51

= 50

= 54   = ?

Answer see page 257

31

The four images follow a pattern. Which option continues the sequence?

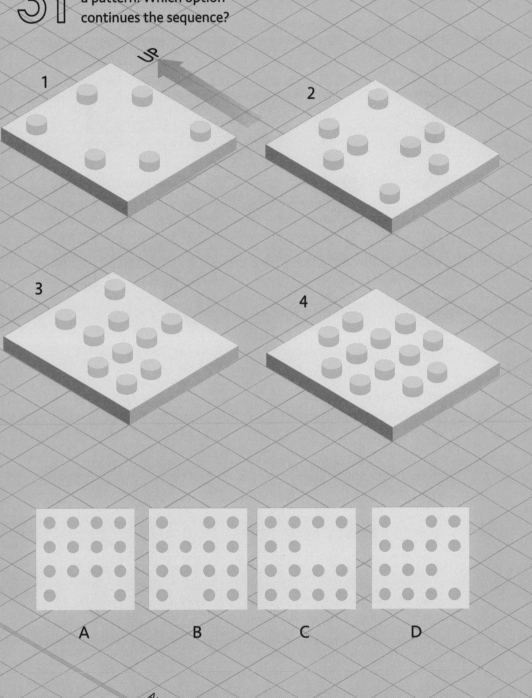

Answer see page 257

32

Rewrite the number 55555, with the addition of just a single line, as 66.

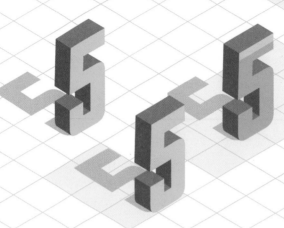

Answer see page 257

Answer see page 257

33

We've given you two separate equations. Each uses the same digits and each of the mathematical operations +, −, x and ÷. Use each of the given numbers to complete each equation. Solve in sequence from left to right – rules regarding the order of mathematical operations do not apply.

6 9 11 12 18

◯ − ◯ x ◯ + ◯ ÷ ◯ = 6

◯ ÷ ◯ x ◯ − ◯ + ◯ = 38

34

The Pharaoh Cleopatra was surrounded by sycophants who fought to be her favourite through fantastic feats of engineering. From the information below, work out who built what in her honour, how long it took to build and to which god it was dedicated.

The magician Dedi's project, which wasn't the pyramid, was dedicated to Isis and took two years more to build than the fortress. The building dedicated to Horus took the most time to build – eight years. Buneb's edifice took half the time it took to build the pyramid, and was dedicated to Amun. The temple, which wasn't overseen by Addaya, most impressed the Pharaoh Cleopatra.

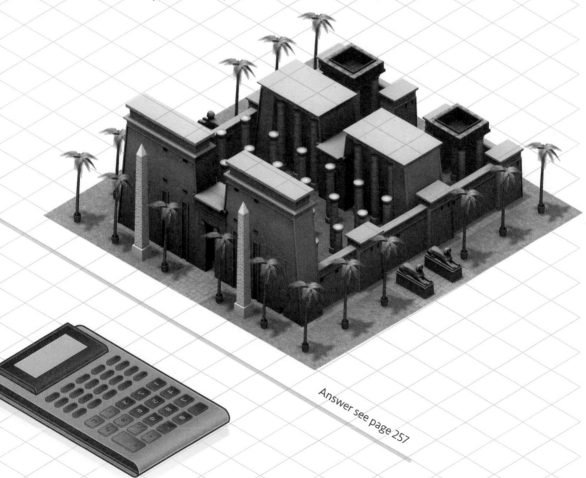

Answer see page 257

35

The first two scales shown are balanced. How many triangles are needed to balance the third?

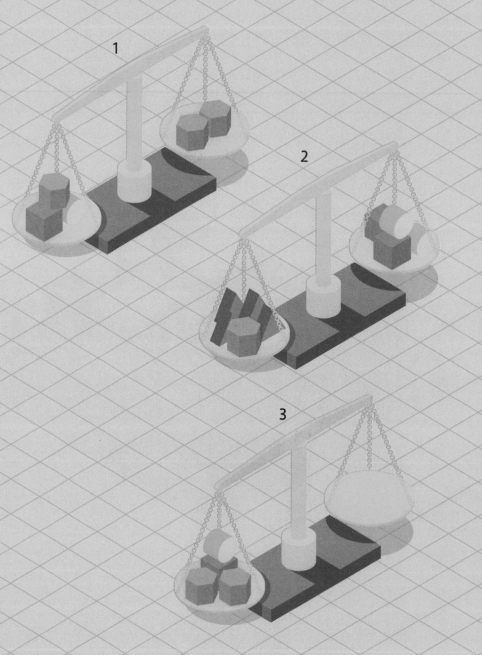

1

2

3

Answer see page 257

36 Each set of numbers represents the name of a famous golfer, the letters of which have been encoded according to the telephone number pad shown. Who are the golfers?

7445642535766
737446427242
522564255287
8443796637
276653725637
76796245769

Answer see page 257

Answer see page 257

37 Identify the mystery number. Compare the information beside the given numbers. Each digit that appears in the mystery number is marked by a dot. Green indicates a digit in the correct position, red if not. Here, 2184 shares three digits with the mystery number, but only two digits are in the correct position.

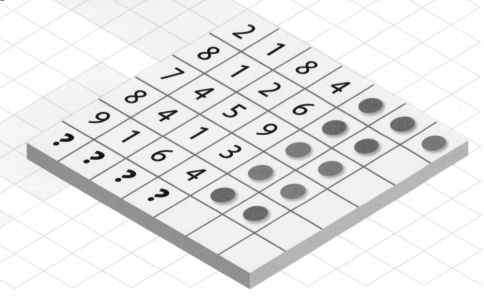

38

All the answers in this "crossword" are numbers. The unclued answer is a date (month, day, year) of significance in clothing.

1	2		3	4		5	6
7		8			9		
	10		11				
12		13	14		15		16
17	18			19			
20			21				
	22				23	24	
25				26		27	
28			29			30	

Across

1 30 Across reversed
3 Descending consecutive numbers
5 First two digits of 17 Across
7 3 Across − 20
9 8 x (6 Down + 1)
10 Hours in a day
11 615 x 15
13 299 + 303 + 308
15 (1 Down + 1) x 9
17 227 x first digit of 3 Across
19 Days in 8 weeks squared
20 A prime number cubed
21 1 Across x first digit of 1 Across
22 23 x 223
23 5 Across x 3
25 Degrees in a circle
26 18 x 31
28 3 x 30 Across
29 28 Across + 14 Down + 25 Down + 30 Across
30 Square root of 16 Down

Down

1 4 x 10 Across
2 24 Down − 21 Across
4 $74^2 + (7 \times 4 \text{ halved})$
5 All different odd numbers
6 First two digits of 16 Down
8 21 Across x 4 Down
9 UNCLUED
12 Anagram of 29 Across
14 Smallest number with exactly six divisors
16 4 Down − 22 Across
18 Sequence of ascending digits
19 First two digits of 19 Across
21 373 x 24
24 20% of 4755
25 Ascending consecutive odd numbers
27 $5^2 + 8^2$

Answer see page 258

39 Which option most accurately completes the pattern?

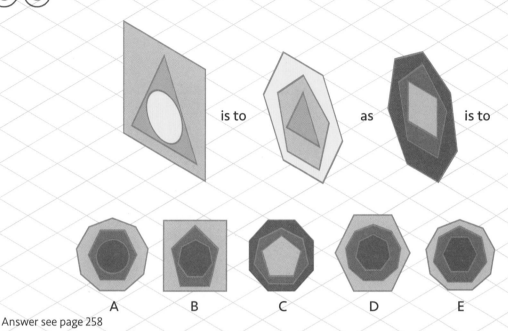

is to ... as ... is to

A   B   C   D   E

Answer see page 258

Answer see page 258

40 Fill the 3x3 grid with each of the listed colours as directed: red, orange, yellow, green, blue, purple, pink, brown, black. All references refer to the same row or column, so that "A is above B" means A and B are in the same column, while "C is to the right/left of D" means C and D are in the same row. Black is below orange and to the left of purple. Green is above both red and brown. Yellow is above purple, which is to the left of brown. Red is to the right of orange and yellow, and blue is to the right of pink.

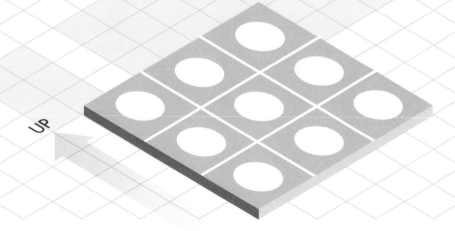

Test 3

01

Place a digit from 1 to 6 into every square, so that no digit repeats in any row or column. Numbers separated by a greater than or less than sign must obey that sign. Arrows always point to the smaller number of a pair.

Answer see page 258

02

Place numbers from 1 to 9 so that each row, column and bold-lined 3x3 box contains one of each number. Numbers from 1 to 3 must be placed in regular grid squares; numbers from 4 to 6 must be placed in grid squares that contain a green circle; and numbers from 7 to 9 must be placed in grid squares that contain an orange circle.

Answer see page 258

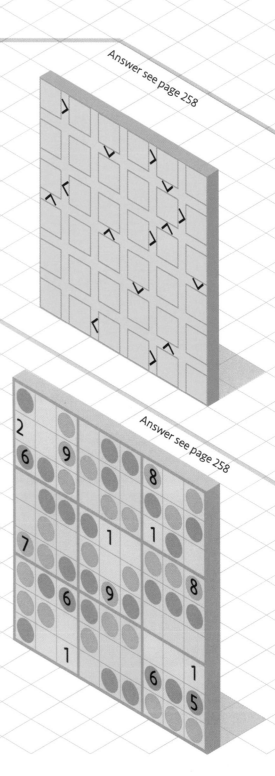

03 Write a number in each empty block so that every block is equal to the sum of the two blocks immediately below it.

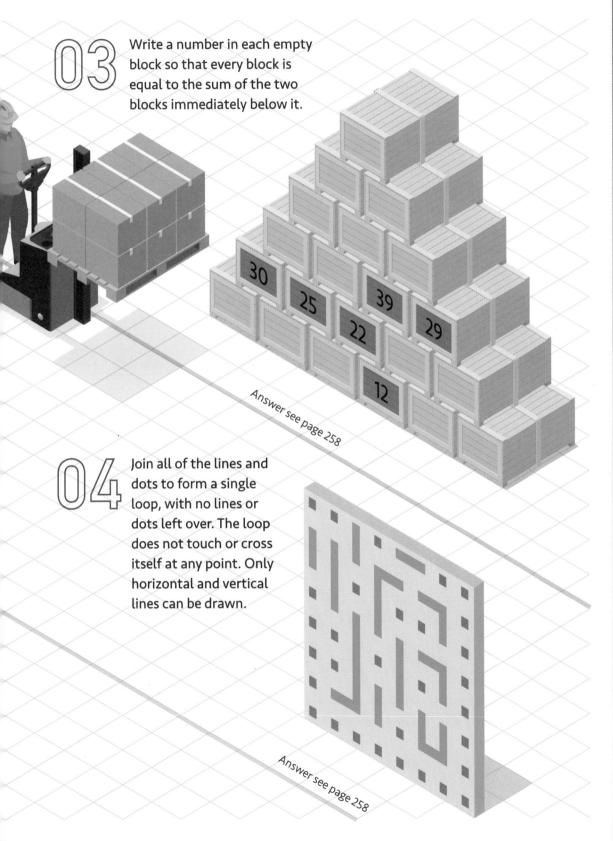

Answer see page 258

04 Join all of the lines and dots to form a single loop, with no lines or dots left over. The loop does not touch or cross itself at any point. Only horizontal and vertical lines can be drawn.

Answer see page 258

05 Place a number from 1 to 7 once each into every row and column of the grid, while obeying the region clues. The value at the top left of each bold-lined region must be obtained when all of the numbers in that region have the given operation (+, −, ×, ÷) applied between them. For − and ÷ operations, begin with the largest number in the region and then subtract or divide by the other numbers in the region in any order.

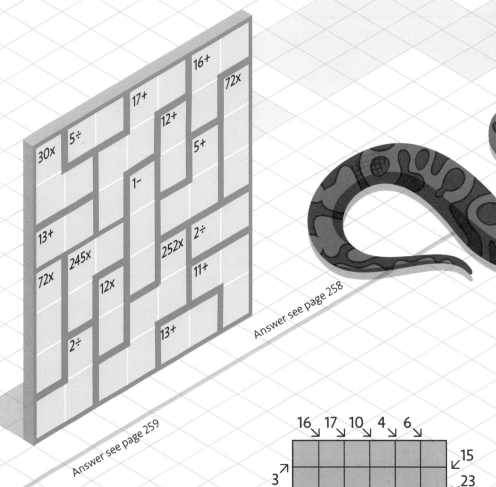

Answer see page 259

Answer see page 258

06 Place a number from 1 to 6 once each in every row and column. Values outside the grid give the total of the numbers in each of the indicated diagonals.

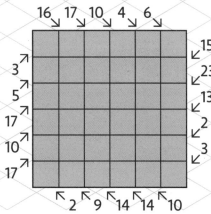

07

Place a colour into each empty square so that every colour appears once in each row, column and bold-lined jigsaw shape.

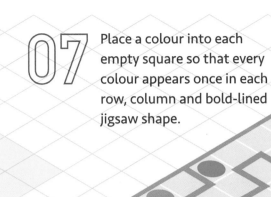

Answer see page 259

08

Shade some squares to form a snake that starts and ends at the snake eyes. Numbers outside the grid specify the number of squares in their row or column that contain part of the snake. A snake is a single path of adjacent shaded squares that does not branch. Shaded squares cannot touch, except for the immediately preceding and following squares in the snake. Shaded squares also cannot touch diagonally, except as necessary for the snake to turn a corner.

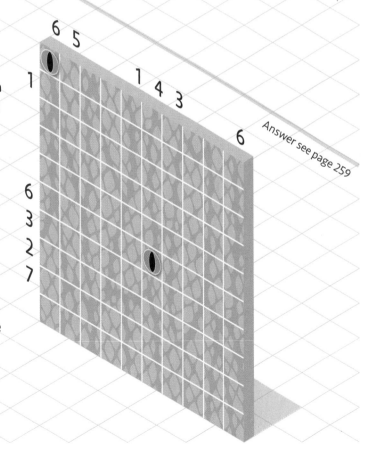

Answer see page 259

09 Draw a single loop by joining some dots so that each numbered square has the specified number of adjacent line segments. Dots can only be joined by horizontal or vertical lines, and the loop cannot touch, cross or overlap itself in any way.

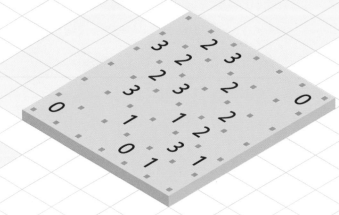

Answer see page 259

10 Draw paths to join pairs of matching coloured shapes. Paths can only travel in straight lines between the centres of squares, and no more than one path can enter any square. Paths cannot touch or cross.

Answer see page 259

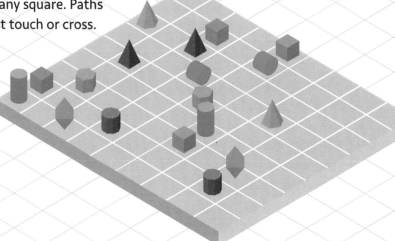

11 Join dots with horizontal and vertical lines to form a single path which does not touch or cross itself at any point. The start and end of the path are given by the red circles. Numbers outside the grid specify the number of dots in their row or column that are visited by the path.

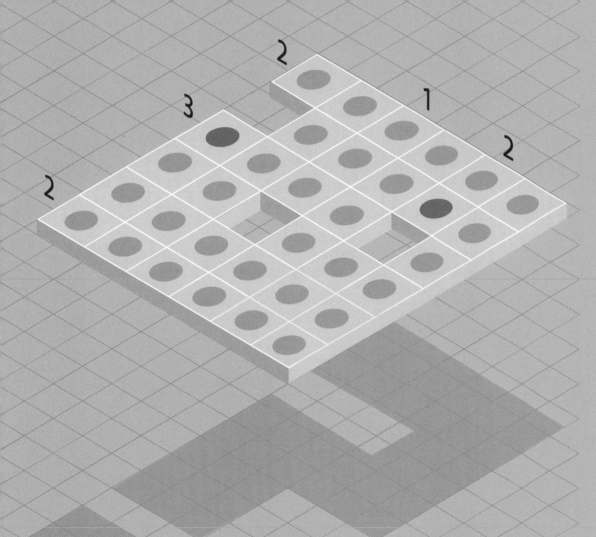

Answer see page 259

12 Place a digit from 1 to 5 into every square, so that no digit repeats in any row or column inside the grid. Place digits in such a way that each given clue number outside the grid represents the number of digits that are "visible" from that point, looking along that clue's row or column. A digit is visible if there is no higher digit preceding it.

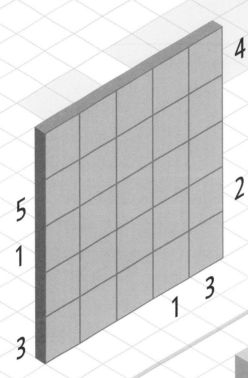

4

5

1

2

3

1 3

3

Answer see page 259

Answer see page 259

13 Place a letter from A to G into every square, so that no letter repeats in any row or column. Identical letters cannot be in diagonally touching squares.

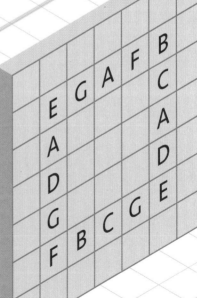

14

Draw along the dashed lines to divide the grid to form a complete set of standard dominoes, with exactly one of each domino. A "0" represents a blank on a traditional domino. Use the check-off chart (right) to help you keep track of which dominoes you've placed.

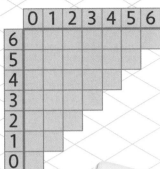

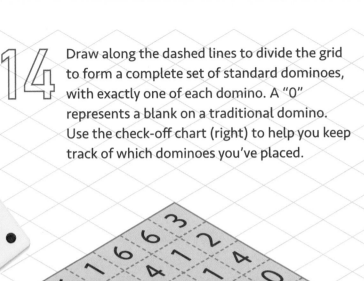

	0	1	2	3	4	5	6
6							
5							
4							
3							
2							
1							
0							

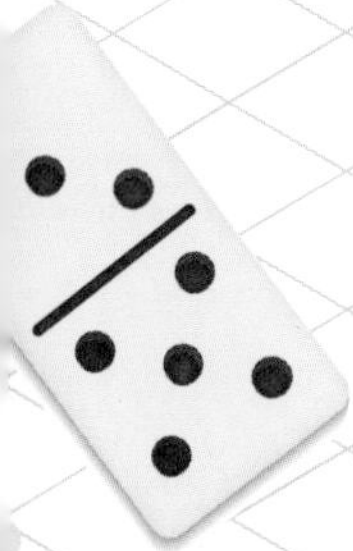

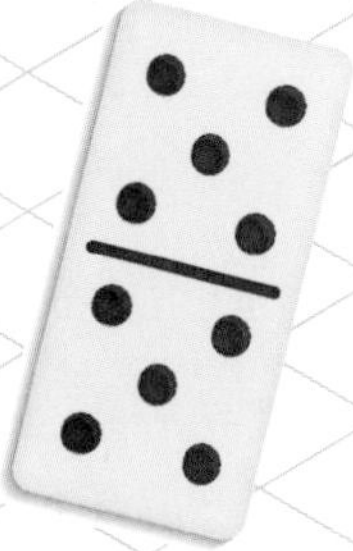

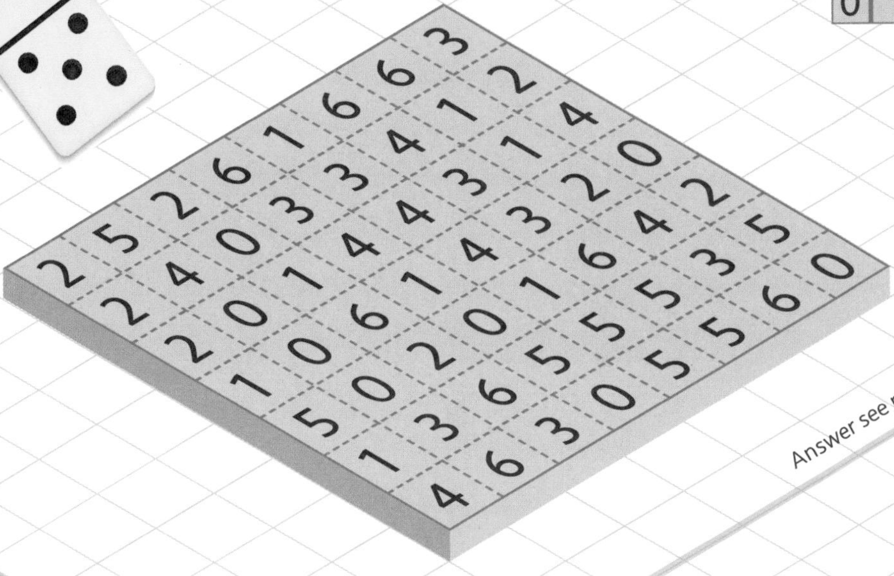

Answer see page 259

Answer see page 259

15

Trace along the dashed lines to divide up the area into four separate pieces. All of the pieces must be identical in shape, although they may be rotated relative to one another. Reflections that are not also rotations are not counted as identical.

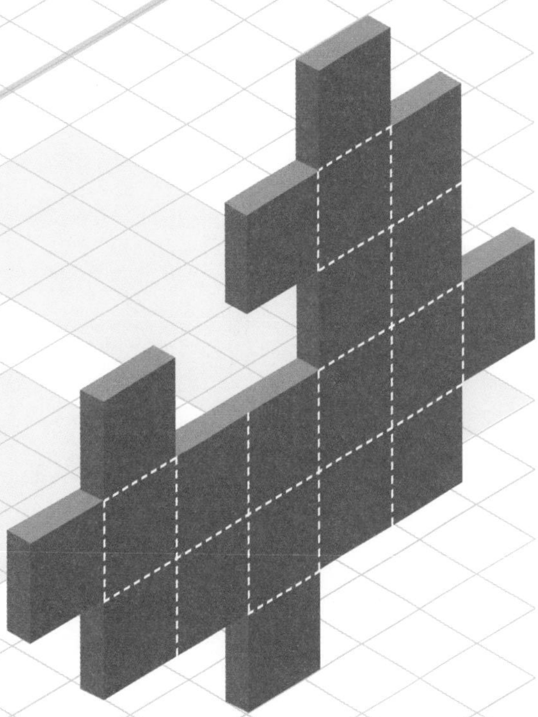

16 Place a digit from 1 to 8 into every square, so that each digit appears once in every row and column. Squares separated by a pink peg must contain two consecutive numbers, such as 2 and 3. Squares separated by a red peg must contain numbers where one is twice the value of the other, such as 2 and 4. All possible dots are given, so if there is no dot, then a neighbouring pair can be neither consecutive nor have one be twice the value of the other. Where 1 and 2 are neighbours, either a red peg or a pink peg might be given, but not both.

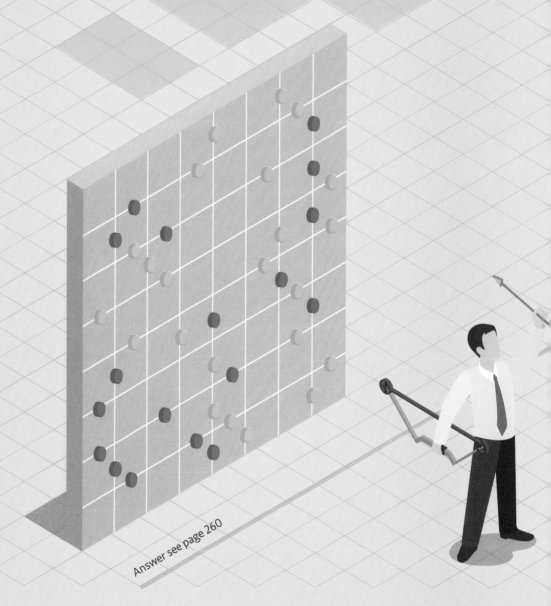

Answer see page 260

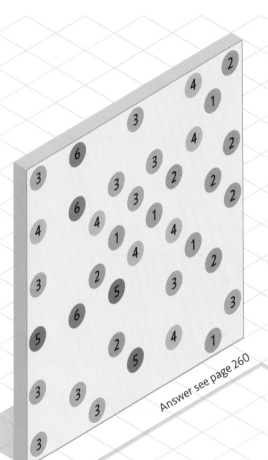

17

Draw horizontal and vertical lines along each row and column of circles to join circled numbers. Each circle contains a number which specifies the number of lines that connect to it. No more than two lines may join any pair of circles. Lines may not cross other lines or circles. All circles must be joined in such a way that you can travel from any circle to any other circle by following one or more lines.

Answer see page 260

18

Can you make each of the totals shown? For each total, choose one number from the outer ring, one number from the middle ring, and one number from the inner ring. The three numbers must add up to the given total.

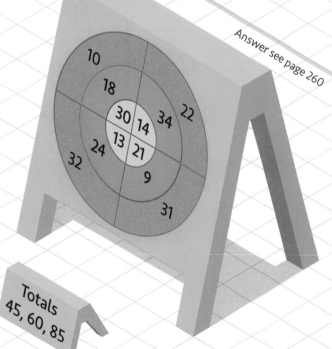

Answer see page 260

Totals
45, 60, 85

19 Place a digit from 1 to 9 into each yellow square, so that no digit repeats in any consecutive horizontal or vertical run of squares. Each horizontal or vertical run has a total given immediately to its left or above, respectively. The digits in that run must add up to the given total.

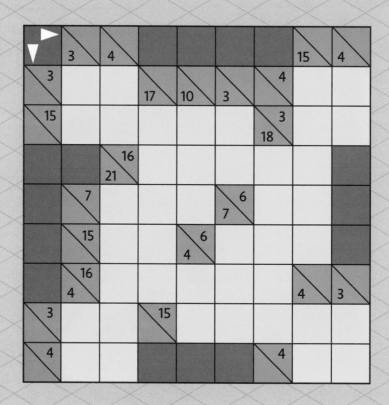

Reveal a hidden picture by shading some squares, while obeying the clues at the start of each row or column. The clues provide, in reading order, the length of every run of consecutive shaded squares in each row and column. There must be a gap of at least one empty square between each run of shaded squares in the same row or column.

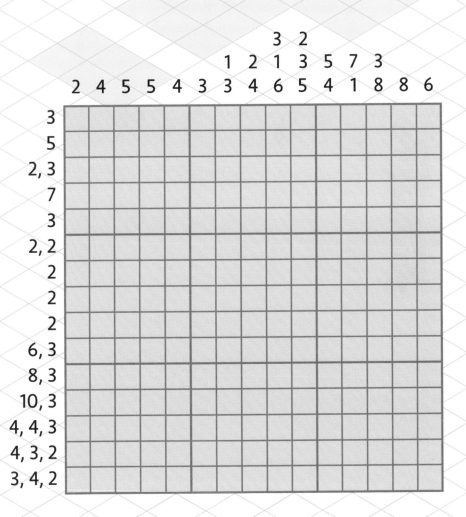

Answer see page 260

21 Write a number in each empty block so that every block is equal to the sum of the two blocks immediately below it.

93

52

18

65

6

Answer see page 260

Answer see page 260

22 One of the numbers given is the sum of two others. How quickly can you locate it?

17   41   37   9   26   22   6   33   14

23

Fill the grid so that each row and column contains the colours red, green and blue, and two empty squares. The coloured digits surrounding the grid indicate which colour is encountered in which positions along that row or column. For example, a green 2 means the second colour encountered moving from the edge of the grid along the row or column is green, while a blue 1 means the first colour encountered is blue.

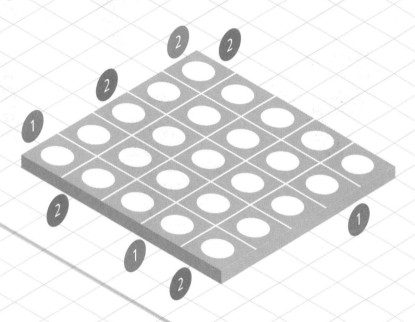

Answer see page 260

24

The planet Centuria has a year that lasts 100 days. Assuming that the chances of being born on any day are equal, how many Centurians need to gather in order for it to be more likely than not that two share the same birthday?

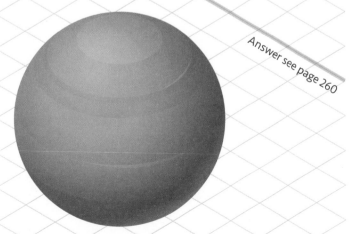

Answer see page 260

25

Three of the four instruments pictured are odd in relation to the other three. Which of the four is a perfect match with the other three?

Flute

Guitar

Violin

Cello

Answer see page 261

Answer see page 261

26

Fill the grid with the digits 1-9 to make the sums work. Solve from left to right and top to bottom in sequence – rules regarding the order of mathematical operations do not apply.

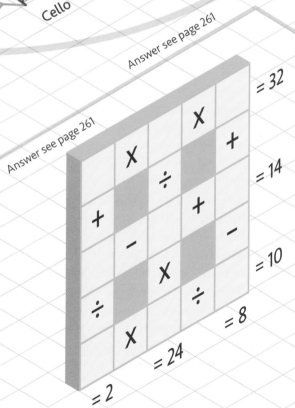

27

Fit the listed numbers into the grid.

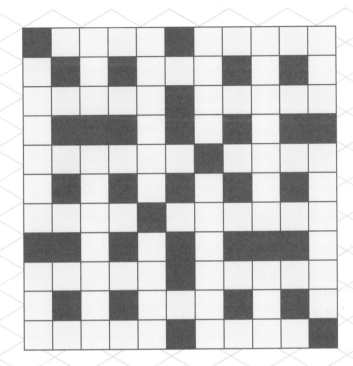

3 digits	4 digits	5 digits	6 digits	7 digits
105	4197	15471	350386	2928463
215	4723	45231	370434	2956483
291	4757	45234	452686	
494	6120	53870	652337	
751	6427	57340	750414	
798	6753	90234	776417	

Answer see page 261

28

What number completes the sequence?

363   224   139   85   54   31   23   ?

Answer see page 261

29

Fill in the blank shape following the below rules:

All squares have moved, but just two of the triangles have changed position. Red is still orthogonally adjacent to three colours, including purple and green. Orange has moved to the bottom half of the grid. Light green is orthogonally adjacent to light blue, which is in a different row. Yellow is still adjacent to orange.

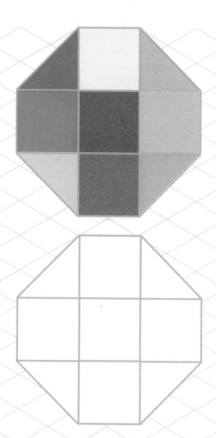

Answer see page 261

30

What is the value represented by the question mark?

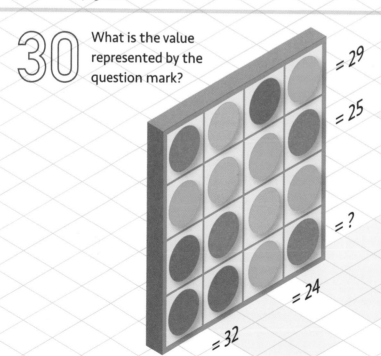

= 29

= 25

= ?

= 24

= 32

Answer see page 261

31 The first two scales shown are balanced. How many triangles are needed to balance the third?

1

2

3

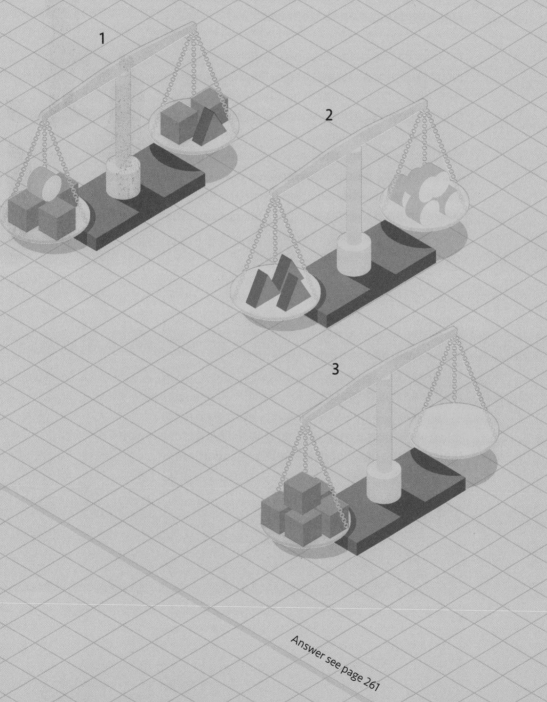

Answer see page 261

32

Three neighbors, quite coincidentally, were retiring on the same day. From the information below, work out how long each had been in their job, the gift they received from their colleagues, and where they planned to travel.

At 33 years, Yuri had spent less time in his job than either of his neighbors. Yehudi, who was hoping to vacation in the Alps, wasn't the neighbor receiving a wristwatch, the male recipient of which wanted to vacation in Rome. Yasmin was retiring after 45 years in her job. She wasn't the person who received the fob watch. Texas was the vacation destination of the neighbor given the carriage clock, who wasn't the neighbor retiring after 40 years.

Answer see page 261

Answer see page 261

33

We've given you two separate equations. Each uses the same digits and each of the mathematical operations +, −, x and ÷. Use each of the given numbers to complete each equation. Solve in sequence from left to right – rules regarding the order of mathematical operations do not apply.

3 4 6 7 28

◯ − ◯ ÷ ◯ x ◯ + ◯ = 46

◯ ÷ ◯ + ◯ − ◯ x ◯ = 92

34

Which option most accurately completes the pattern?

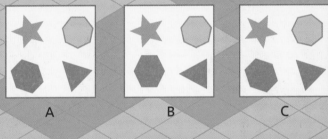

is to ... as ... is to

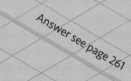

A   B   C

D   E

Answer see page 261

35 The four images follow a pattern. Which option continues the sequence?

1

2

3

4

A   B   C   D

Answer see page 261

36 Each set of numbers represents the name of a U.S. president, the letters of which have been encoded according to the telephone number pad shown. Who are the presidents?

87867
62262
732426
227837
466837
26654343

Answer see page 261

Answer see page 261

37 Fill the 3x3 grid with each of the listed colours as directed: red, orange, yellow, green, blue, purple, pink, brown, black. All references refer to the same row or column, so that "A is above B" means A and B are in the same column, while "C is to the right/left of D" means C and D are in the same row. Pink is above both orange and yellow, which is to the left of purple. Green, to the left of red and pink, is above black. Purple is below both red and brown, which is to the right of black. Blue is to the left of yellow.

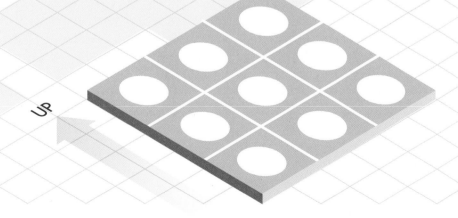

38 All the answers in this "crossword" are numbers. The unclued answer is a date (month, day, year) of significance in sports.

Across

1 $1907 \times 2^3 \times 3^3$
6 Square root of 20 Down
7 6 Down ÷ 10 Across
8 241 + 271 + 281
10 One third of 23 Across
11 421 + 431 + 431
12 18 Down x 19 Across
14 Anagram of 19 Down
15 Add 1 to each digit of 6 Down
17 66,083 x 7 Across
19 5432 – 4342
21 Half of 19 Down
22 27 x 28
23 20% of 6 Down
24 8 Across ÷ 13
25 10 Across x 11 Across x 5

Down

1 6 Across + 10
2 17 Across + 25 Across
3 16 Down – 5 Down
4 16 x 17
5 6 Down + 21 Across
6 Ascending consecutive numbers
9 17 x 32 x 181
10 6 Down – 23 Across
11 UNCLUED
13 7 Across x 24 Across x 23 Down
16 300% of 19 Down
18 6 Down + 19 Down
19 11 x 16
20 222 + 314 + 425
23 Last two digits of 19 Down reversed
24 $4^2 + 7^2$

Answer see page 261

39

(Largest prime number below 100 – spots on two dice) + (Colours of the rainbow x planets in the solar system)

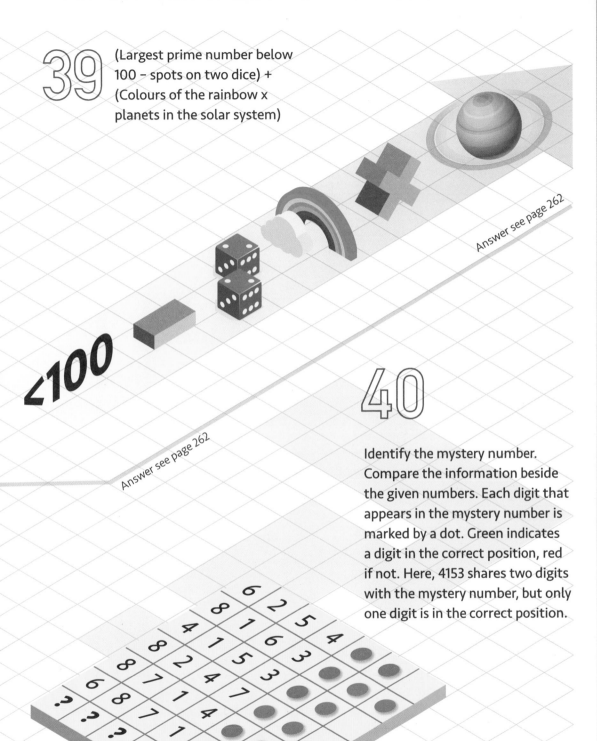

Answer see page 262

‹100

Answer see page 262

40

Identify the mystery number. Compare the information beside the given numbers. Each digit that appears in the mystery number is marked by a dot. Green indicates a digit in the correct position, red if not. Here, 4153 shares two digits with the mystery number, but only one digit is in the correct position.

Test 4

01 Place a digit from 1 to 6 into every square, so that no digit repeats in any row or column. Numbers separated by a greater than or less than sign must obey that sign. Arrows always point to the smaller number of a pair.

Answer see page 262

02 Place numbers from 1 to 9 so that each row, column and bold-lined 3x3 box contains one of each number. Numbers from 1 to 3 must be placed in regular grid squares; numbers from 4 to 6 must be placed in grid squares that contain a green circle; and numbers from 7 to 9 must be placed in grid squares that contain an orange circle.

Answer see page 262

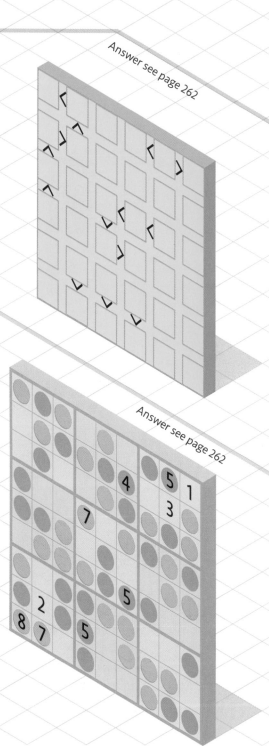

03

Write a number in each empty block so that every block is equal to the sum of the two blocks immediately below it.

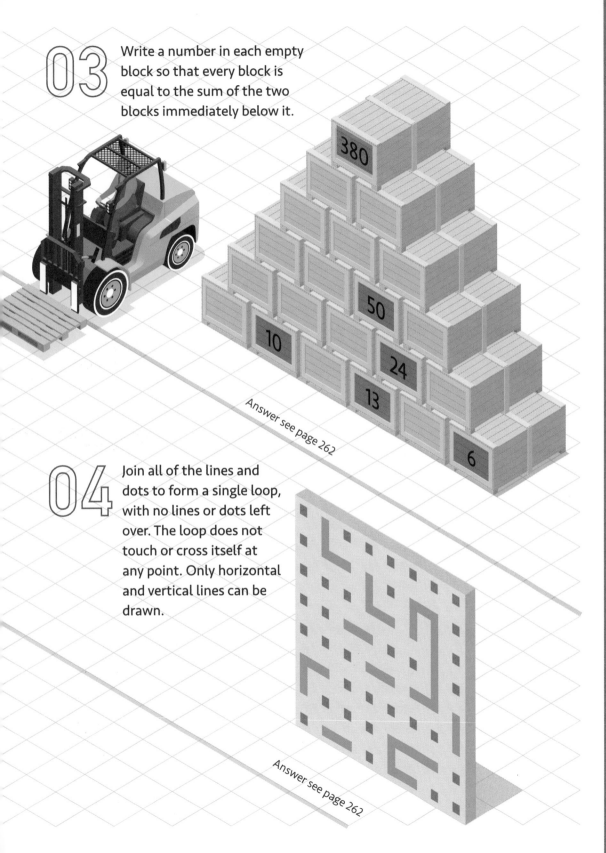

380

50

10

24

13

6

Answer see page 262

04

Join all of the lines and dots to form a single loop, with no lines or dots left over. The loop does not touch or cross itself at any point. Only horizontal and vertical lines can be drawn.

Answer see page 262

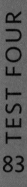

05

Place a number from 1 to 7 once each into every row and column of the grid, while obeying the region clues. The value at the top left of each bold-lined region must be obtained when all of the numbers in that region have the given operation (+, −, ×, ÷) applied between them. For − and ÷ operations, begin with the largest number in the region and then subtract or divide by the other numbers in the region in any order.

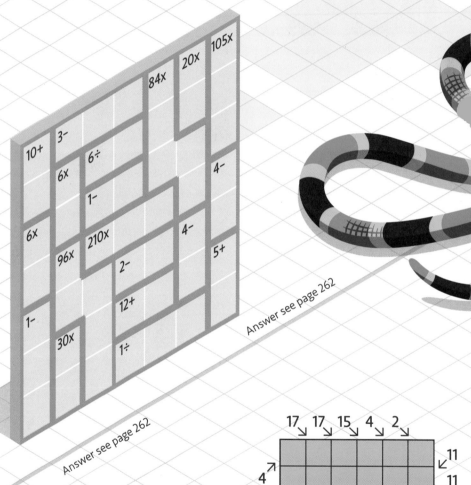

Answer see page 262

06

Place a number from 1 to 6 once each in every row and column. Values outside the grid give the total of the numbers in each of the indicated diagonals.

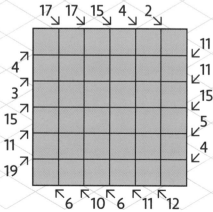

07

Place a colour into each empty square so that every colour appears once in each row, column and bold-lined jigsaw shape.

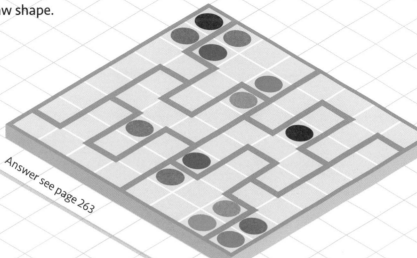

Answer see page 263

08

Shade some squares to form a snake that starts and ends at the snake eyes. Numbers outside the grid specify the number of squares in their row or column that contain part of the snake. A snake is a single path of adjacent shaded squares that does not branch. Shaded squares cannot touch, except for the immediately preceding and following squares in the snake. Shaded squares also cannot touch diagonally, except as necessary for the snake to turn a corner.

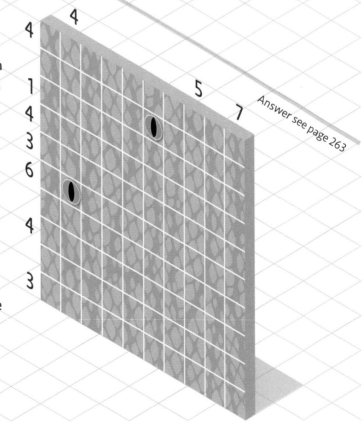

Answer see page 263

Draw a single loop by joining some dots so that each numbered square has the specified number of adjacent line segments. Dots can only be joined by horizontal or vertical lines, and the loop cannot touch, cross or overlap itself in any way.

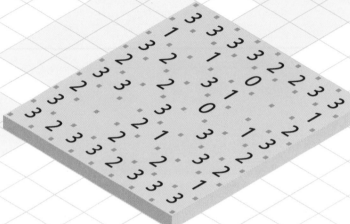

Answer see page 263

10 Draw paths to join pairs of matching coloured shapes. Paths can only travel in straight lines between the centres of squares, and no more than one path can enter any square. Paths cannot touch or cross.

Answer see page 263

11 Join dots with horizontal and vertical lines to form a single path which does not touch or cross itself at any point. The start and end of the path are given by the red circles. Numbers outside the grid specify the number of dots in their row or column that are visited by the path.

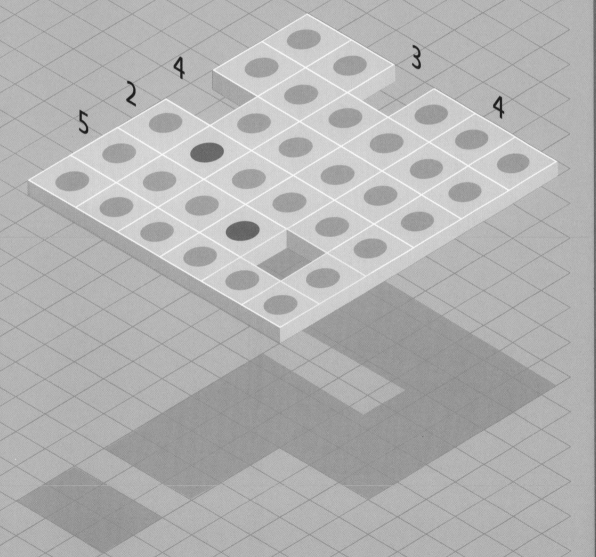

Answer see page 263

12 Place a digit from 1 to 5 into every square, so that no digit repeats in any row or column inside the grid. Place digits in such a way that each given clue number outside the grid represents the number of digits that are "visible" from that point, looking along that clue's row or column. A digit is visible if there is no higher digit preceding it.

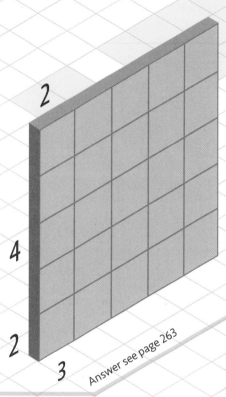

Answer see page 263

13 Place a letter from A to G into every square, so that no letter repeats in any row or column. Identical letters cannot be in diagonally touching squares.

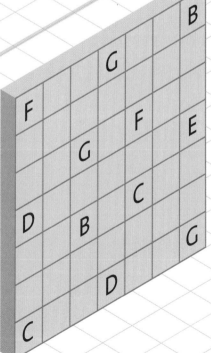

Answer see page 263

14 Draw along the dashed lines to divide the grid to form a complete set of standard dominoes, with exactly one of each domino. A "0" represents a blank on a traditional domino. Use the check-off chart (right) to help you keep track of which dominoes you've placed.

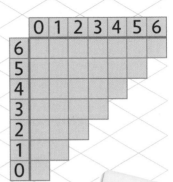

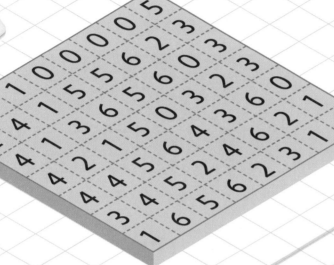

Answer see page 263

Answer see page 263

15 Trace along the dashed lines to divide up the area into three separate pieces. All of the pieces must be identical in shape, although they may be rotated relative to one another. Reflections that are not also rotations are not counted as identical.

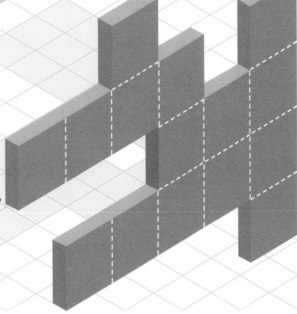

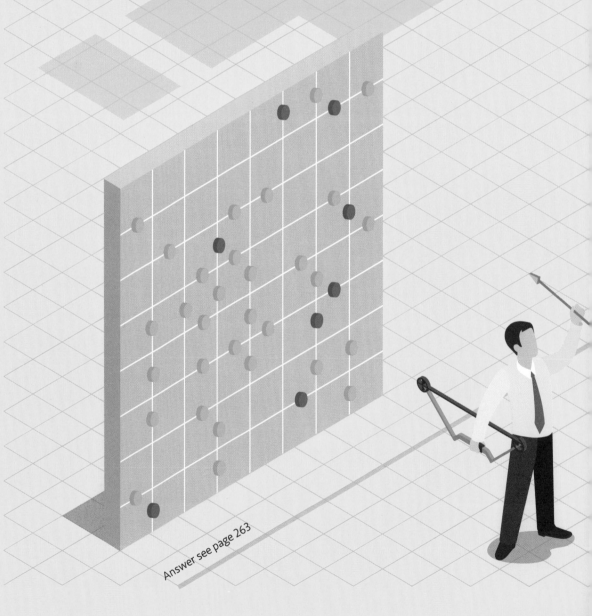

16 Place a digit from 1 to 8 into every square, so that each digit appears once in every row and column. Squares separated by a pink peg must contain two consecutive numbers, such as 2 and 3. Squares separated by a red peg must contain numbers where one is twice the value of the other, such as 2 and 4. All possible dots are given, so if there is no dot, then a neighbouring pair can be neither consecutive nor have one be twice the value of the other. Where 1 and 2 are neighbours, either a red peg or a pink peg might be given, but not both.

Answer see page 263

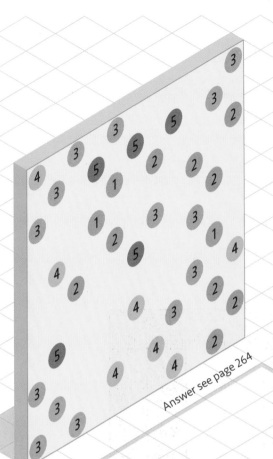

Answer see page 264

17

Draw horizontal and vertical lines along each row and column of circles to join circled numbers. Each circle contains a number which specifies the number of lines that connect to it. No more than two lines may join any pair of circles. Lines may not cross other lines or circles. All circles must be joined in such a way that you can travel from any circle to any other circle by following one or more lines.

Answer see page 264

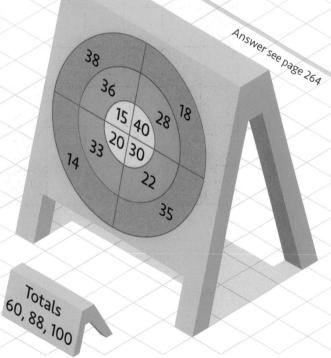

18

Can you make each of the totals shown? For each total, choose one number from the outer ring, one number from the middle ring, and one number from the inner ring. The three numbers must add up to the given total.

Totals
60, 88, 100

19 Place a digit from 1 to 9 into each yellow square, so that no digit repeats in any consecutive horizontal or vertical run of squares. Each horizontal or vertical run has a total given immediately to its left or above, respectively. The digits in that run must add up to the given total.

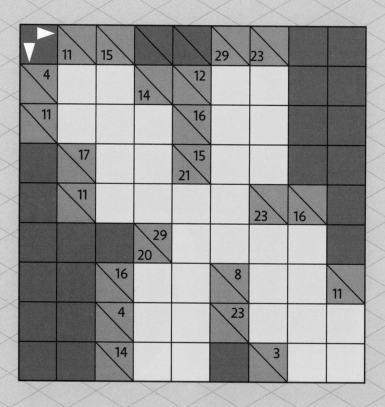

Answer see page 264

Reveal a hidden picture by shading some squares, while obeying the clues at the start of each row or column. The clues provide, in reading order, the length of every run of consecutive shaded squares in each row and column. There must be a gap of at least one empty square between each run of shaded squares in the same row or column.

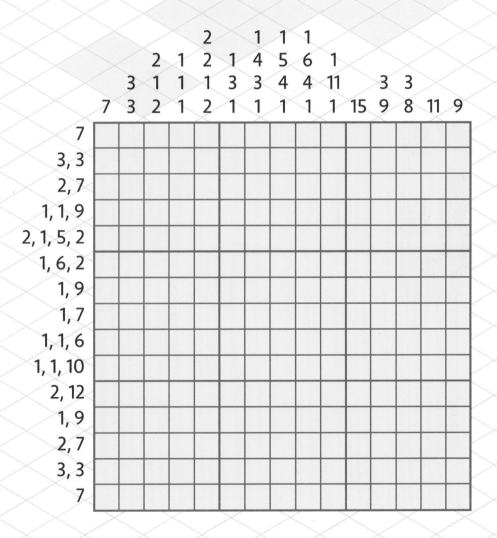

Answer see page 264

21

Write a number in each empty block so that every block is equal to the sum of the two blocks immediately below it.

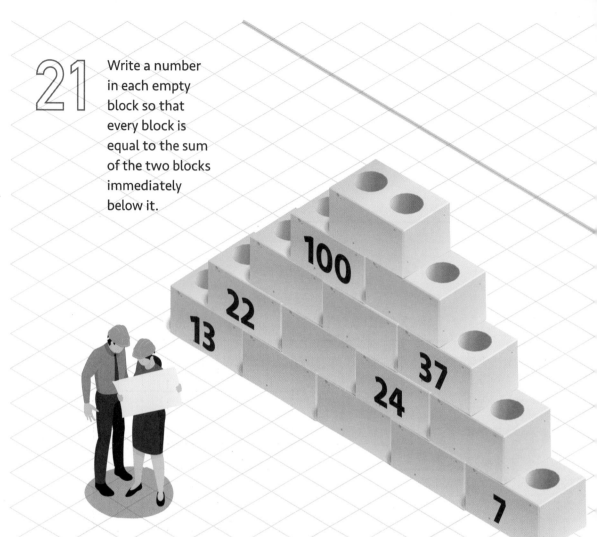

Answer see page 264

Answer see page 264

22

One of the numbers given is the sum of two others. How quickly can you locate it?

19 18 17 9 4 25 12 14 24

23 Identify the mystery number. Compare the information beside the given numbers. Each digit that appears in the mystery number is marked by a dot. Green indicates a digit in the correct position, red if not. Here, 8326 shares two digits with the mystery number, but only one digit is in the correct position.

Answer see page 264

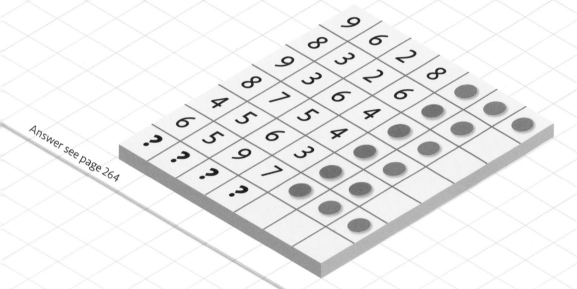

24 What is the value of yellow?

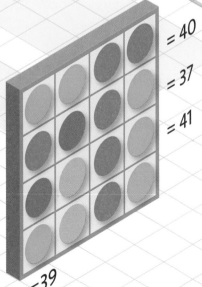

= 40

= 37

= 41

= 39

Answer see page 264

25 Three of the four deities pictured are odd in relation to the other three. Which of the four is a perfect match with the other three?

Venus

Uranus

Cupid

Jupiter

Answer see page 264

Answer see page 264

26 Fill the grid with the digits 1-9 to make the sums work. Solve from left to right and top to bottom in sequence – rules regarding the order of mathematical operations do not apply.

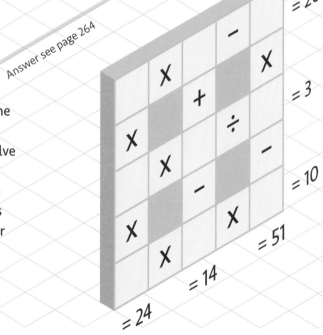

= 20

= 3

= 10

= 51

= 14

= 24

27

What number completes the sequence?

10   12   9   14   7   18   ?

Answer see page 265

Answer see page 265

28

Fit the listed numbers into the grid.

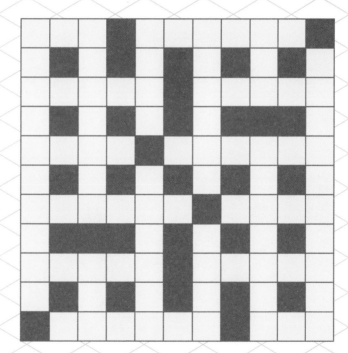

3 digits	4 digits	5 digits	6 digits	7 digits	10 digits
120	1458	36575	123794	5743215	1234987690
155	1654	63042	296587	5751236	2234087699
599	3458	63256	321584		
920	9628	94175	396620		
			603784		
			706894		

29

Fill in the blank shape following the below rules:

Four hexagons have changed position, one of the striped hexagons has not. The pale blue and yellow hexagons are adjacent to just the red striped hexagon.

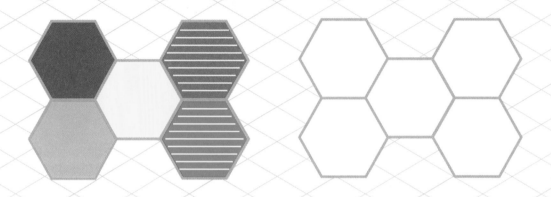

Answer see page 265

Answer see page 265

30

(Roman D ÷ Roman CXXV) x (Number of players in a basketball team + countries in Central America)

31

The four images follow
a pattern. Which option
continues the sequence?

1

2

3

4

A   B   C   D

Answer see page 265

32

All the answers in this "crossword" are numbers. The unclued answer is a date (month, day, year) of significance in acting.

Across

1 Whole weeks in a year
3 2.5% of 12 Down
5 2^4
7 149 x 2 x 3 x 7
9 2 Down + 26 Down - 10
11 UNCLUED
13 Product of two prime numbers
14 13 Down + 15 Down + 24 Down
16 47 x 303
17 53 x 6
19 15 Down – 1 Across – 27 Across
21 8 Down – 10 Down + 400,000
24 9 x 11 x 24 Down
25 73,021 ÷ first two digits of 18 Down
27 4% of 950
28 Descending consecutive numbers
29 Freezing point of water in degrees Fahrenheit

Down

1 1288 ÷ 24 Down
2 (5 Across -1) x 149
3 26 Down reversed x 18
4 9^3
5 5 Across x 11^2
6 First two digits of 14 Across, reversed
8 587,983 x 9
10 13 Down x 24 Down squared x 27 Across
12 6092 + 6093 + 6095
13 1 Across + 24 Down + 27 Across
15 2 x 5 x 7 x 9
18 27 Across reversed x 5 Across
20 3 Across x 3^2
22 $3^2 + 4^2 + 5^2 + 6^2 + 7^2 + 8^2 + 9^2 - 1$
23 28 Across – 15 Down
24 29 Across reversed
26 1 Down + 5 Across

33 Three people were standing at a bus stop on December 27. As they got chatting, they discovered that they were all returning an unwanted Christmas gift to the shops from which they were bought. From the information given, work out who returned which gift to which store and how much they received as a refund.

Veronica wasn't the woman returning the (hopelessly unflattering) dress. The unwanted laptop was refunded $299, which was more than the camera, but not to Maurice, who was the recipient of the $199 refund. The cheapest gift, refunded $129, wasn't returned to Favourites. Herbert Wilson refunded more than Lewis John refunded Lucinda.

Answer see page 265

Answer see page 265

34 Fill the 3x3 grid with each of the listed colours as directed: red, orange, yellow, green, blue, purple, pink, brown, black. All references refer to the same row or column, so that "A is above B" means A and B are in the same column, while "C is to the right/left of D" means C and D are in the same row. Green, above pink, is to the right of brown, which is above purple. Black is to the right of red, which is below blue. Orange is above blue, which is to the left of purple and pink. Green is above yellow, which is to the right of red and black.

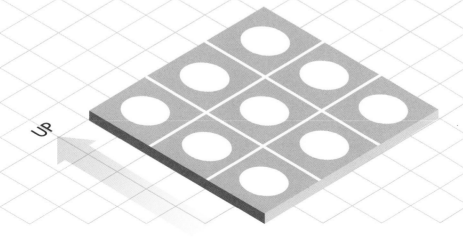

UP

35

The president's husband has a reputation for being thrifty. He has just two sets of seven pairs of socks, and each pair of socks in a set is a different colour of the rainbow. Getting ready for a weekend away, and packing in the dark, how many individual socks does the president's husband need to take from the drawer to guarantee a matching pair will be packed? How many more socks need to be packed to ensure a second matching pair of socks?

Answer see page 265

36

We've given you two separate equations. Each uses the same digits and each of the mathematical operations +, −, x and ÷. Use each of the given numbers to complete each equation. Solve in sequence from left to right – rules regarding the order of mathematical operations do not apply.

Answer see page 265

4 5 7 8 15

$$\bigcirc - \bigcirc \times \bigcirc + \bigcirc \div \bigcirc = 8$$

$$\bigcirc \div \bigcirc \times \bigcirc + \bigcirc - \bigcirc = 28$$

37

Which option most accurately completes the pattern?

1010 is to **10** as **1111** is to

12 A

13 B

14 C

15 D

16 E

Answer see page 265

38 The first two scales
shown are balanced.
What needs to be
added to the third to
balance the scales?

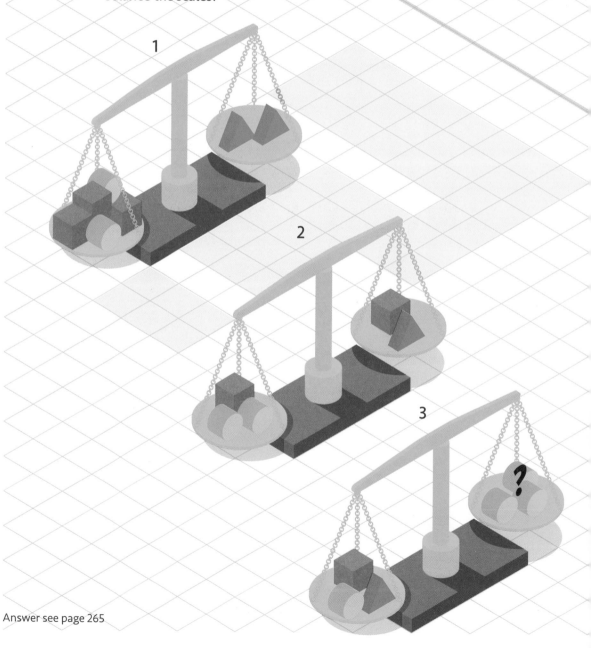

1

2

3

Answer see page 265

39

Each set of numbers represents the name of a non-native, English-speaking, Oscar-winning actor, the letters of which have been encoded according to the telephone number pad shown. What are the names?

2 3 6 4 2 4 6 3 3 5 8 6 7 6
7 6 2 3 7 8 6 2 3 6 4 4 6 4
5 3 2 6 3 8 5 2 7 3 4 6
2 4 7 4 7 8 6 7 4 9 2 5 8 9
5 2 8 4 3 7 2 2 7 3 3 6

Answer see page 265

40

Fill the grid so that each row and column contains the colours red, green and blue, and two empty squares. The coloured digits surrounding the grid indicate which colour is encountered in which positions along that row or column. For example, a blue 1 means the first colour encountered moving from the edge of the grid along the row or column is blue, while a green 2 means the second colour encountered is green.

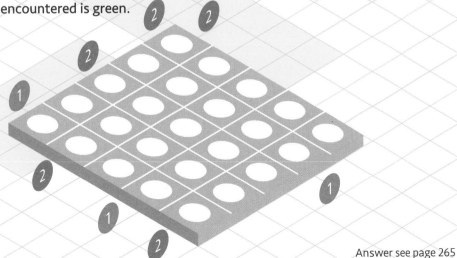

Answer see page 265

Test 5

01

Place a digit from 1 to 6 into every square, so that no digit repeats in any row or column. Numbers separated by a greater than or less than sign must obey that sign. Arrows always point to the smaller number of a pair.

Answer see page 266

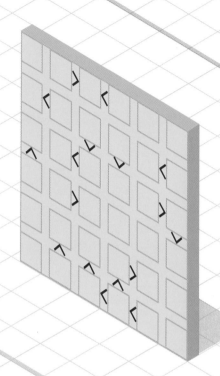

02

Draw paths to join pairs of matching coloured shapes. Paths can only travel in straight lines between the centres of squares, and no more than one path can enter any square. Paths cannot touch or cross.

Answer see page 266

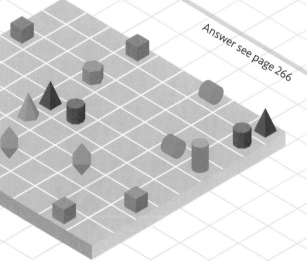

03 Write a number in each empty block so that every block is equal to the sum of the two blocks immediately below it.

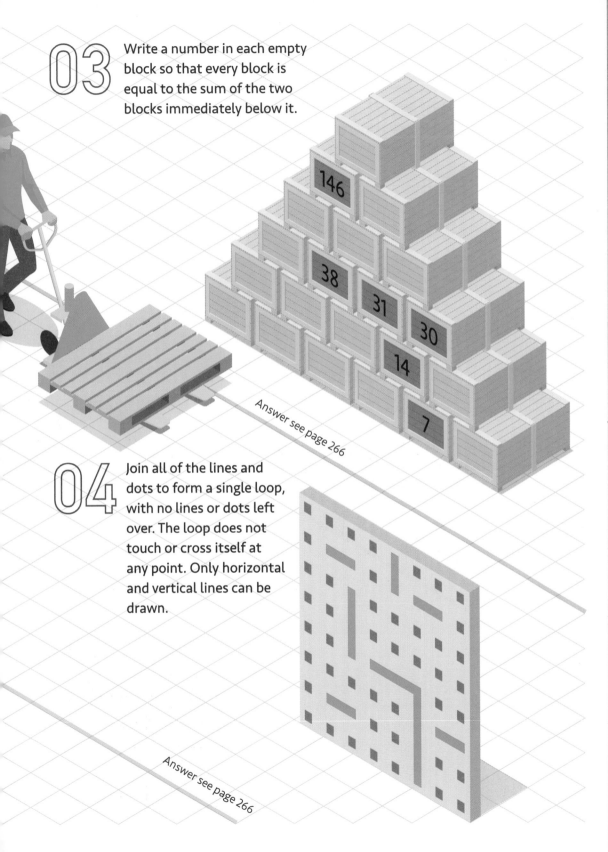

146

38

31

30

14

7

Answer see page 266

04 Join all of the lines and dots to form a single loop, with no lines or dots left over. The loop does not touch or cross itself at any point. Only horizontal and vertical lines can be drawn.

Answer see page 266

05 Place a number from 1 to 7 once each into every row and column of the grid, while obeying the region clues. The value at the top left of each bold-lined region must be obtained when all of the numbers in that region have the given operation (+, −, ×, ÷) applied between them. For − and ÷ operations, begin with the largest number in the region and then subtract or divide by the other numbers in the region in any order.

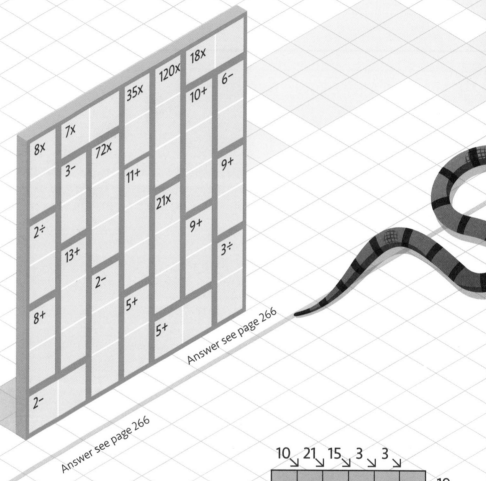

Answer see page 266

Answer see page 266

06 Place a number from 1 to 6 once each in every row and column. Values outside the grid give the total of the numbers in each of the indicated diagonals.

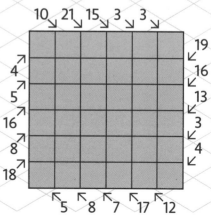

07 Place a colour into each empty square so that every colour appears once in each row, column and bold-lined jigsaw shape.

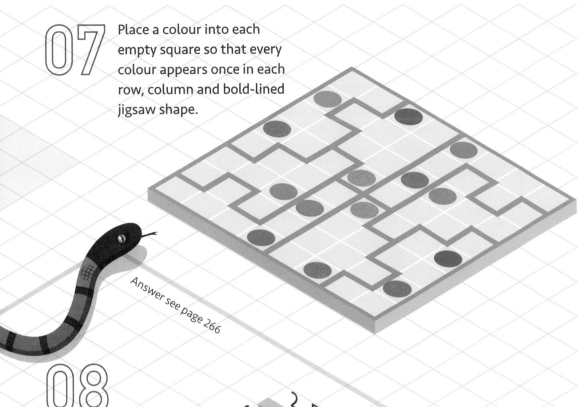

Answer see page 266

08

Shade some squares to form a snake that starts and ends at the snake eyes. Numbers outside the grid specify the number of squares in their row or column that contain part of the snake. A snake is a single path of adjacent shaded squares that does not branch. Shaded squares cannot touch, except for the immediately preceding and following squares in the snake. Shaded squares also cannot touch diagonally, except as necessary for the snake to turn a corner.

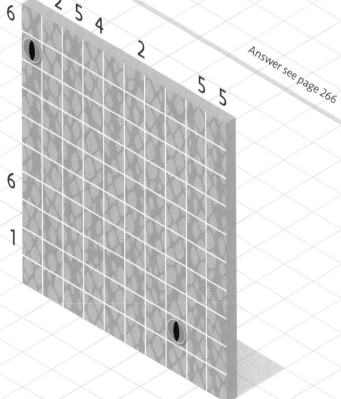

Answer see page 266

09 Place a digit from 1 to 5 into every square, so that no digit repeats in any row or column inside the grid. Place digits in such a way that each given clue number outside the grid represents the number of digits that are "visible" from that point, looking along that clue's row or column. A digit is visible if there is no higher digit preceding it.

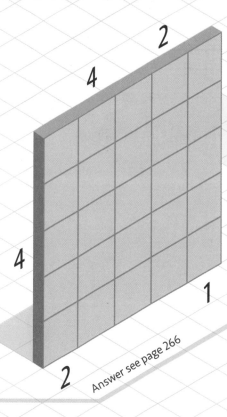

Answer see page 266

10 Trace along the dashed lines to divide up the area into four separate pieces. All of the pieces must be identical in shape, although they may be rotated relative to one another. Reflections that are not also rotations are not counted as identical.

Answer see page 267

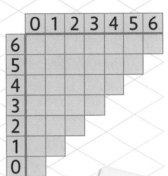

11 Draw along the dashed lines to divide the grid to form a complete set of standard dominoes, with exactly one of each domino. A "0" represents a blank on a traditional domino. Use the check-off chart (right) to help you keep track of which dominoes you've placed.

	0	1	2	3	4	5	6
6							
5							
4							
3							
2							
1							
0							

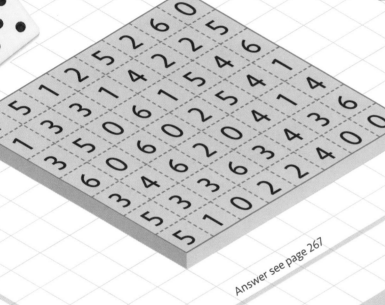

Answer see page 267

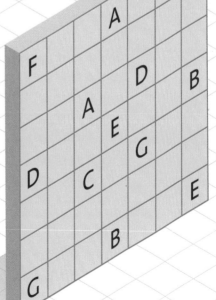

12 Place a letter from A to G into every square, so that no letter repeats in any row or column. Identical letters cannot be in diagonally touching squares.

Answer see page 267

13 Draw a single loop by joining some dots so that each numbered square has the specified number of adjacent line segments. Dots can only be joined by horizontal or vertical lines, and the loop cannot touch, cross or overlap itself in any way.

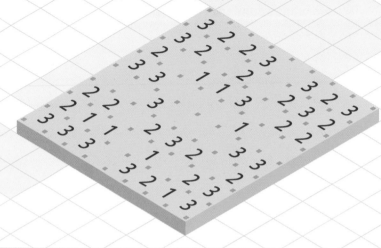

Answer see page 267

Answer see page 267

14 Place numbers from 1 to 9 so that each row, column and bold-lined 3x3 box contains one of each number. Numbers from 1 to 3 must be placed in regular grid squares; numbers from 4 to 6 must be placed in grid squares that contain a green circle; and numbers from 7 to 9 must be placed in grid squares that contain an orange circle.

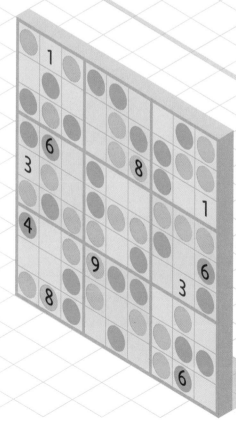

15 Join dots with horizontal and vertical lines to form a single path which does not touch or cross itself at any point. The start and end of the path are given by the red circles. Numbers outside the grid specify the number of dots in their row or column that are visited by the path.

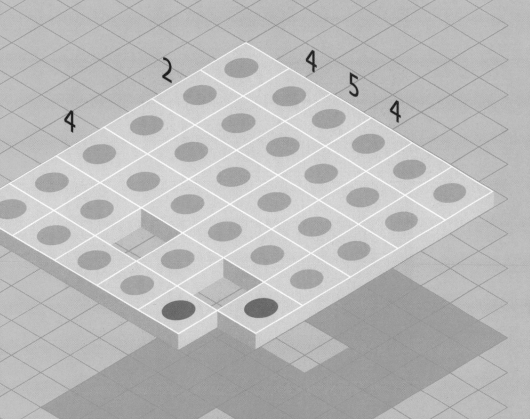

Answer see page 267

16

Place a digit from 1 to 9 into each yellow square, so that no digit repeats in any consecutive horizontal or vertical run of squares. Each horizontal or vertical run has a total given immediately to its left or above, respectively. The digits in that run must add up to the given total.

17 Reveal a hidden picture by shading some squares, while obeying the clues at the start of each row or column. The clues provide, in reading order, the length of every run of consecutive shaded squares in each row and column. There must be a gap of at least one empty square between each run of shaded squares in the same row or column.

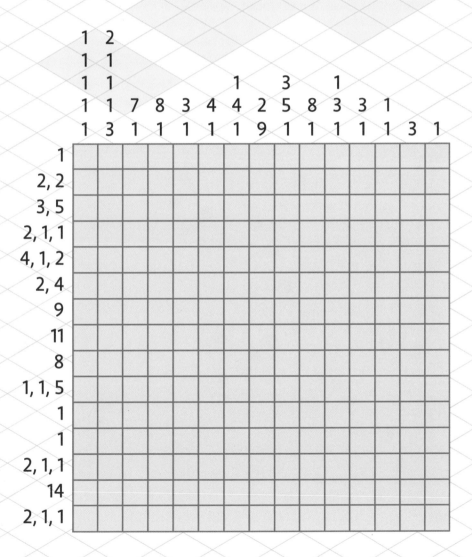

Answer see page 267

18

Place a digit from 1 to 8 into every square, so that each digit appears once in every row and column. Squares separated by a pink peg must contain two consecutive numbers, such as 2 and 3. Squares separated by a red peg must contain numbers where one is twice the value of the other, such as 2 and 4. All possible dots are given, so if there is no dot, then a neighbouring pair can be neither consecutive nor have one be twice the value of the other. Where 1 and 2 are neighbours, either a red peg or a pink peg might be given, but not both.

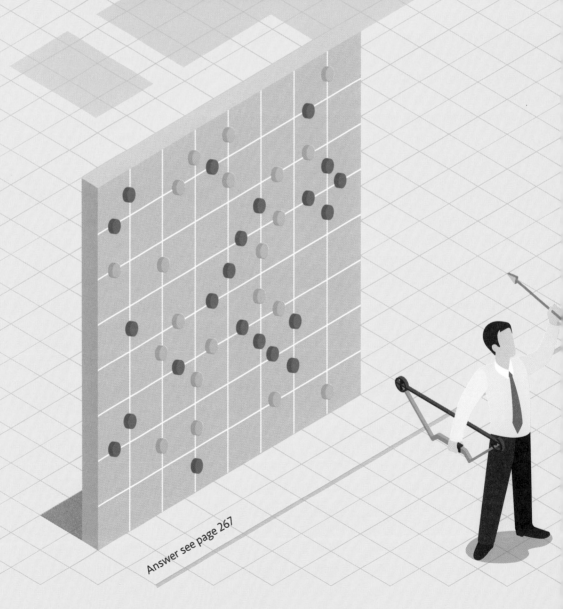

Answer see page 267

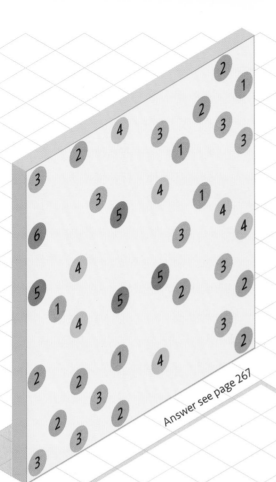

19 Draw horizontal and vertical lines along each row and column of circles to join circled numbers. Each circle contains a number which specifies the number of lines that connect to it. No more than two lines may join any pair of circles. Lines may not cross other lines or circles. All circles must be joined in such a way that you can travel from any circle to any other circle by following one or more lines.

Answer see page 267

Answer see page 268

20 Can you make each of the totals shown? For each total, choose one number from the outer ring, one number from the middle ring, and one number from the inner ring. The three numbers must add up to the given total.

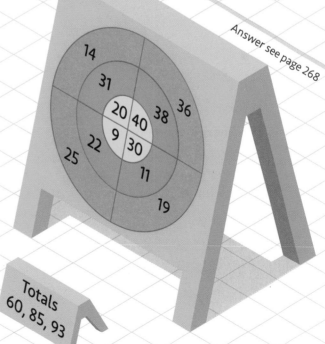

Totals
60, 85, 93

21

Write a number in each empty block so that every block is equal to the sum of the two blocks immediately below it.

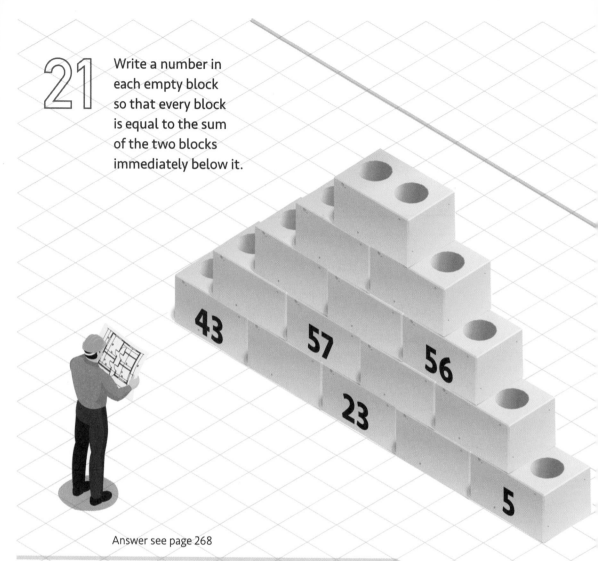

43   57   56

23

5

Answer see page 268

Answer see page 268

22

One of the numbers given is the sum of two others. How quickly can you locate it?

23   16   33   9   12   28   38   27   20

23 Fill the grid so that each row and column contains the colours red, green and blue, and two empty squares. The coloured digits surrounding the grid indicate which colour is encountered in which positions along that row or column. For example, a green 1 means the first colour encountered moving from the edge of the grid along the row or column is green, while a blue 2 means the second colour encountered is blue.

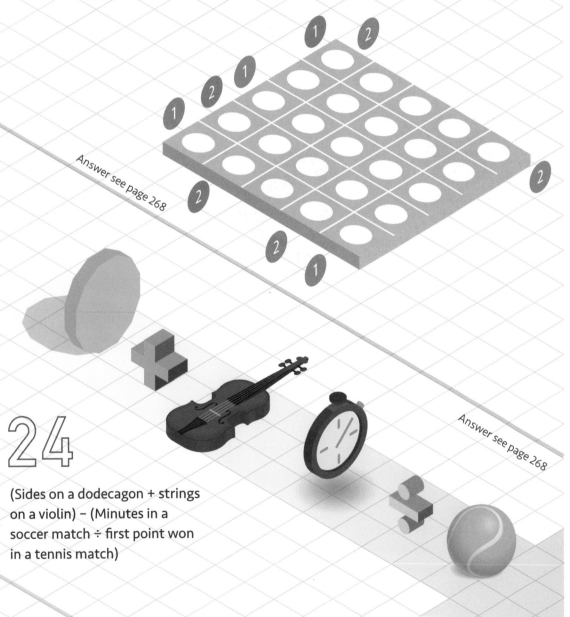

Answer see page 268

Answer see page 268

24 (Sides on a dodecagon + strings on a violin) − (Minutes in a soccer match ÷ first point won in a tennis match)

25 Three of the four names given are odd in relation to the other three. Which of the four is a perfect match with the other three?

Romeo

Juliet

Oliver

Oscar

Answer see page 268

26 Fill the grid with the digits 1-9 to make the sums work. Solve from left to right and top to bottom in sequence – rules regarding the order of mathematical operations do not apply.

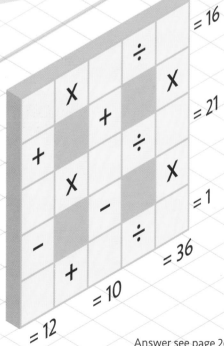

= 16

= 21

= 1

= 36

= 10

= 12

Answer see page 268

27

What number completes
the sequence?

9 21 39 63 93 ?

Answer see page 268

Answer see page 268

28

Fit the listed numbers
into the grid.

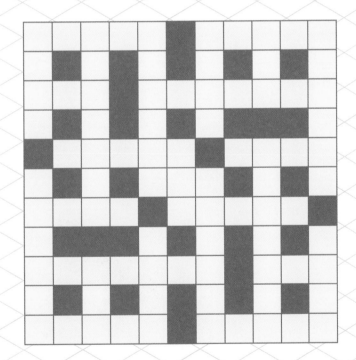

3 digits	4 digits	5 digits	6 digits	7 digits
208	3149	23189	834052	5340724
276	3710	25832	834956	6283541
278	3745	63189	834959	7183521
426	6725	63488	845032	9243700
437	6752	65632		
591	6945	65698		

29 Fill in the blank shape following the below rules:

The yellow triangle is the only one that has not moved position. The blue triangle is between purple and pink, and the red triangle is between green and yellow.

Answer see page 268

30 What is the value of pink?

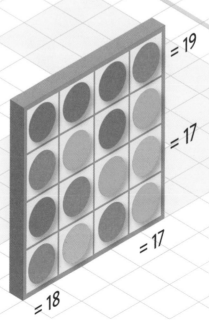

= 19

= 17

= 17

= 18

Answer see page 268

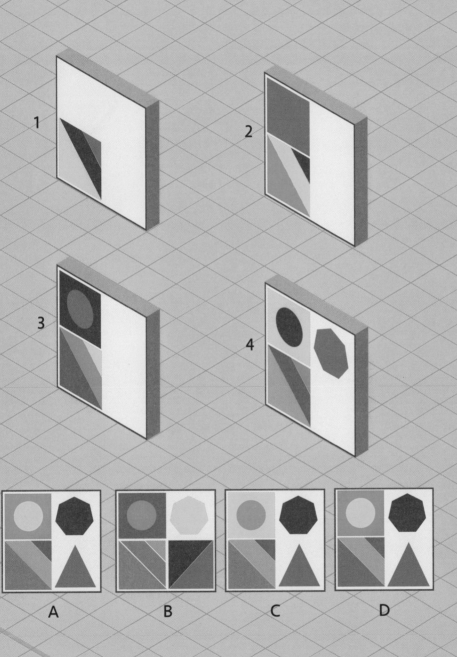

31

The four images follow
a pattern. Which option
continues the sequence?

1

2

3

4

A   B   C   D

Answer see page 268

32

At the Central Conservation Club, the keepers had a daily routine of delivering presents to beasties celebrating birthdays. Today, Suki the seahorse received no presents while Eddie the eagle received 6. Carla the crab was luckier, receiving 30 presents, and Bobbie the butterfly received 18. When the keepers reached Ruby the rhinoceros, how many presents did they deliver?

Answer see page 269

33

We've given you two separate equations. Each uses the same digits and each of the mathematical operations +, −, x and ÷. Use each of the given numbers to complete each equation. Solve in sequence from left to right – rules regarding the order of mathematical operations do not apply.

Answer see page 269

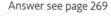
2 3 4 12 24

◯ ÷ ◯ + ◯ − ◯ x ◯ = 48

◯ ÷ ◯ + ◯ x ◯ − ◯ = 33

34

Three contestants – identical triplets – were playing for their teams in the final round of *Chase A Million*, TV's latest and greatest quiz show. From the information below, work out which contestant was on which team, how they styled their hair to show their individuality, how many questions they answered, and how much they contributed to their team's prize fund.

Cora, who wasn't on the green team, answered a total of fifteen questions, and the representative of the yellow team had a ponytail. The person whose contribution to her team was $10,000, not Dora, had a bob. Nora, on the yellow team, wasn't the person adding $5,000 to her team's prize fund, nor was she the contestant who answered twelve questions. The contestant with the cropped hair wasn't the one who answered seven questions, nor was she the contestant on the purple team. The green team's prize pot increased by $5,000, $3,000 less than the yellow team's fund.

Answer see page 269

35 The first three scales shown are balanced. How many cubes are needed to balance the fourth?

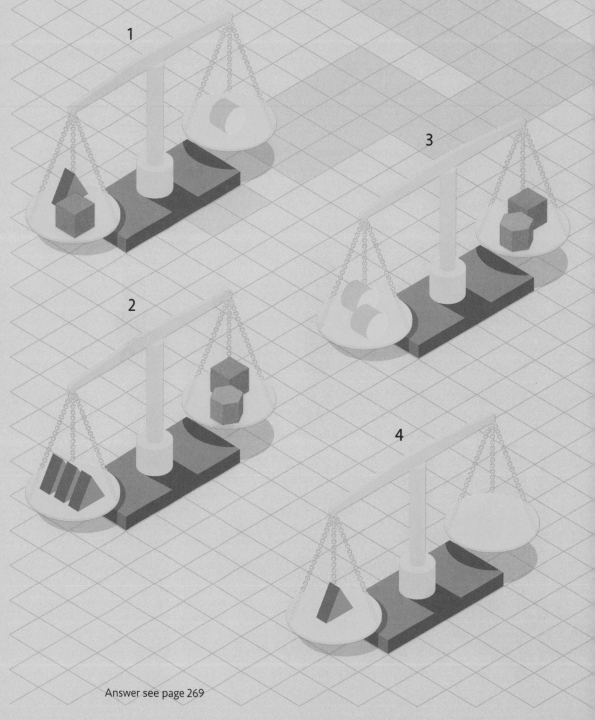

1

2

3

4

Answer see page 269

Each set of numbers represents the name of a one-time only Wimbledon Ladies' champion, the letters of which have been encoded according to the telephone number pad shown. What are the names?

6274273826878
847446429233
2662448262784639
6278462446447
52626686862
62742742727682
26354362873766
6274662278654

Answer see page 269

Answer see page 269

Identify the mystery number. Compare the information beside the given numbers. Each digit that appears in the mystery number is marked by a dot. Green indicates a digit in the correct position, red if not. Here, 4178 shares two digits with the mystery number, but only one digit is in the correct position.

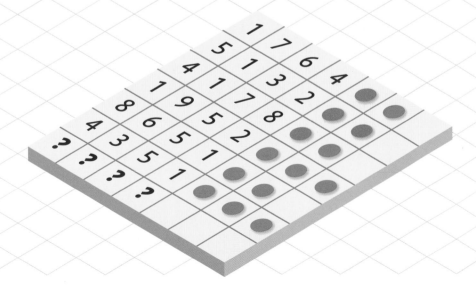

38

All the answers in this "crossword" are numbers. The unclued answer is a date (month, day, year) of significance in comics.

Across

1 6 Across – 22 Down
3 123 + 234 + 22 Down
5 First two digits of 3 Across
6 3 Across – 20 Down
8 Largest two-digit prime number
10 23 Across – 15 Down
13 17 x 29
14 Sum of digits is 33
16 4 Down squared
18 Ascending consecutive digits
19 57 x 613
21 4 Down x 29
23 2121^2
25 Last two digits of 19 Down, reversed
27 26 Down x 6
28 $3^2 + 5^2$
29 13 Across – 6 Across
30 First digit of 29 Across to the power 5 x last two digits of 29 Across

Down

1 UNCLUED
2 3 Across + 30 Across
3 2^2 x 17 x 619
4 1862 ÷ 25 Across
5 125 + 319
7 3^6
9 116,700 ÷ 150
11 3 Across x 22 Down
12 Anagram of 11 Down
15 5 Down x 9 Down
17 A palindrome
19 Half of 9 Down
20 31 + 37 + 41 + 43 + 47
22 $7^2 + 8^2 + 1$
24 19 Down + 434
26 3 Across – 19 Down

Answer see page 269

39

Which option most accurately completes the pattern?

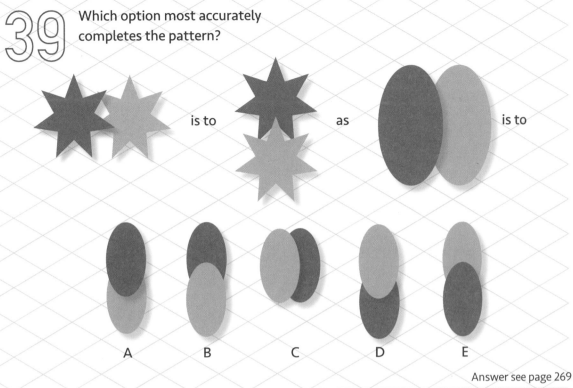

is to ... as ... is to

A   B   C   D   E

Answer see page 269

Answer see page 269

40

Fill the 3x3 grid with each of the listed colours as directed: red, orange, yellow, green, blue, purple, pink, brown, black. All references refer to the same row or column, so that "A is above B" means A and B are in the same column, while "C is to the right/left of D" means C and D are in the same row. Yellow, to the left of brown, is above green. Orange is to the left of black and red and above purple. Purple is above pink, and brown and black are above blue. Green is below red and to the right of pink.

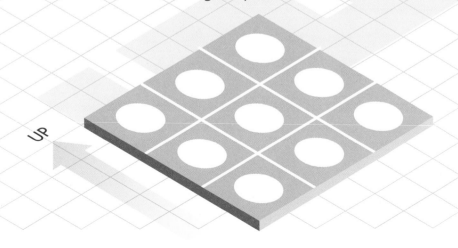

UP

Test 6

01

Place a digit from 1 to 6 into every square, so that no digit repeats in any row or column. Numbers separated by a greater than or less than sign must obey that sign. Arrows always point to the smaller number of a pair.

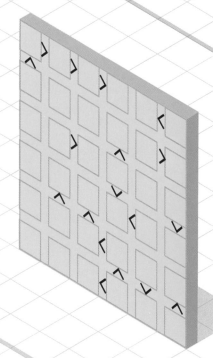

Answer see page 269

02

Draw paths to join pairs of matching coloured shapes. Paths can only travel in straight lines between the centres of squares, and no more than one path can enter any square. Paths cannot touch or cross.

Answer see page 269

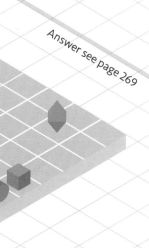

03

Write a number in each empty block so that every block is equal to the sum of the two blocks immediately below it.

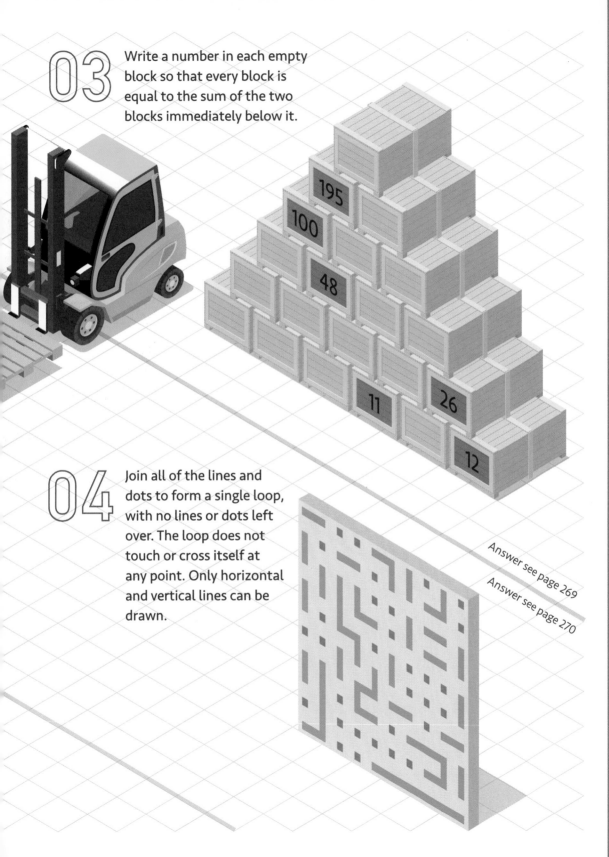

195

100

48

11

26

12

04

Join all of the lines and dots to form a single loop, with no lines or dots left over. The loop does not touch or cross itself at any point. Only horizontal and vertical lines can be drawn.

Answer see page 269

Answer see page 270

05 Place a number from 1 to 7 once each into every row and column of the grid, while obeying the region clues. The value at the top left of each bold-lined region must be obtained when all of the numbers in that region have the given operation (+, −, ×, ÷) applied between them. For − and ÷ operations, begin with the largest number in the region and then subtract or divide by the other numbers in the region in any order.

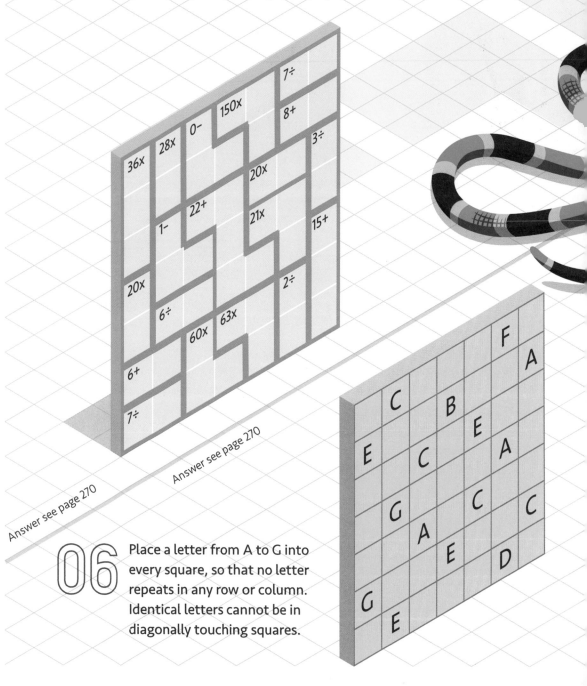

Answer see page 270

Answer see page 270

06 Place a letter from A to G into every square, so that no letter repeats in any row or column. Identical letters cannot be in diagonally touching squares.

07 Place a colour into each empty square so that every colour appears once in each row, column and bold-lined jigsaw shape.

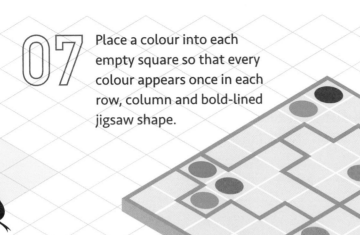

Answer see page 270

08

Shade some squares to form a snake that starts and ends at the snake eyes. Numbers outside the grid specify the number of squares in their row or column that contain part of the snake. A snake is a single path of adjacent shaded squares that does not branch. Shaded squares cannot touch, except for the immediately preceding and following squares in the snake. Shaded squares also cannot touch diagonally, except as necessary for the snake to turn a corner.

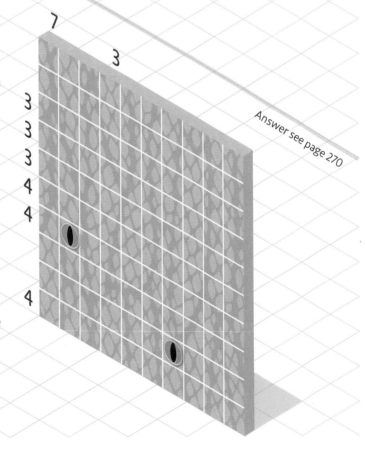

Answer see page 270

Place a digit from 1 to 5 into every square, so that no digit repeats in any row or column inside the grid. Place digits in such a way that each given clue number outside the grid represents the number of digits that are "visible" from that point, looking along that clue's row or column. A digit is visible if there is no higher digit preceding it.

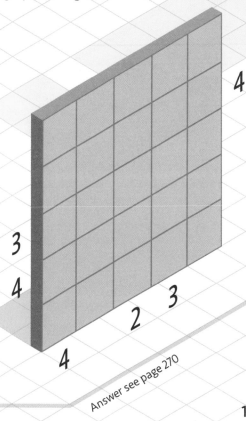

4

3

4

2   3

4

Answer see page 270

Answer see page 270

Place a number from 1 to 7 once each in every row and column. Values outside the grid give the total of the numbers in each of the indicated diagonals.

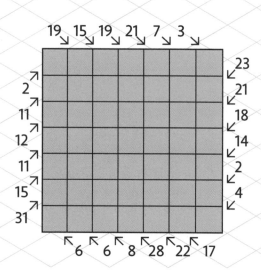

11 Draw along the dashed lines to divide the grid to form a complete set of standard dominoes, with exactly one of each domino. A "0" represents a blank on a traditional domino. Use the check-off chart (right) to help you keep track of which dominoes you've placed.

	0	1	2	3	4	5	6
6							
5							
4							
3							
2							
1							
0							

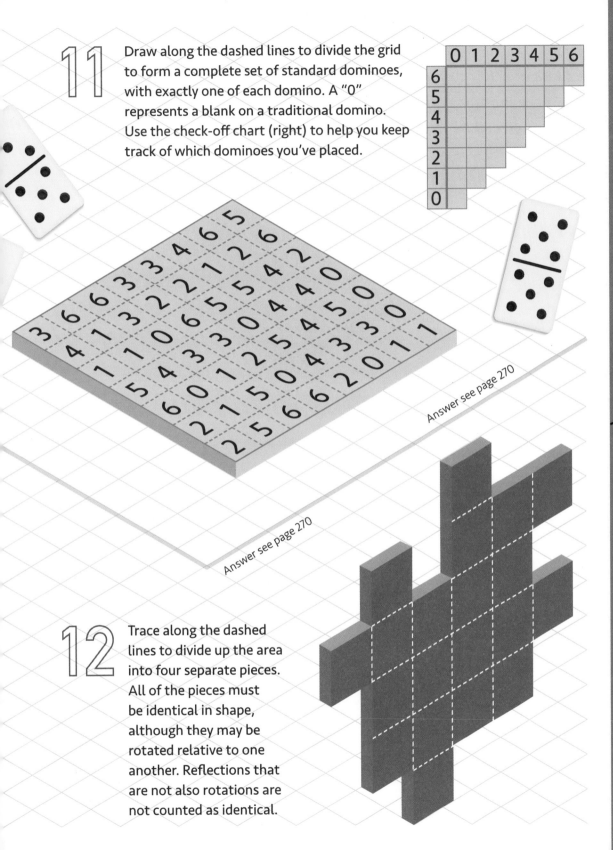

Answer see page 270

Answer see page 270

12 Trace along the dashed lines to divide up the area into four separate pieces. All of the pieces must be identical in shape, although they may be rotated relative to one another. Reflections that are not also rotations are not counted as identical.

13 Draw a single loop by joining some dots so that each numbered square has the specified number of adjacent line segments. Dots can only be joined by horizontal or vertical lines, and the loop cannot touch, cross or overlap itself in any way.

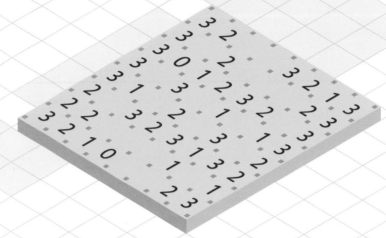

Answer see page 271

Answer see page 271

14 Place numbers from 1 to 9 so that each row, column and bold-lined 3x3 box contains one of each number. Numbers from 1 to 3 must be placed in regular grid squares; numbers from 4 to 6 must be placed in grid squares that contain a green circle; and numbers from 7 to 9 must be placed in grid squares that contain an orange circle.

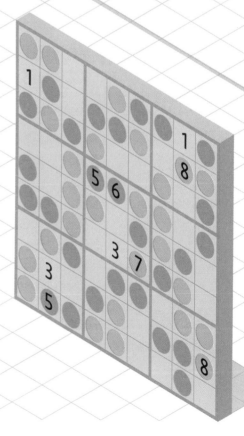

15 Join dots with horizontal and vertical lines to form a single path which does not touch or cross itself at any point. The start and end of the path are given by the red circles. Numbers outside the grid specify the number of dots in their row or column that are visited by the path.

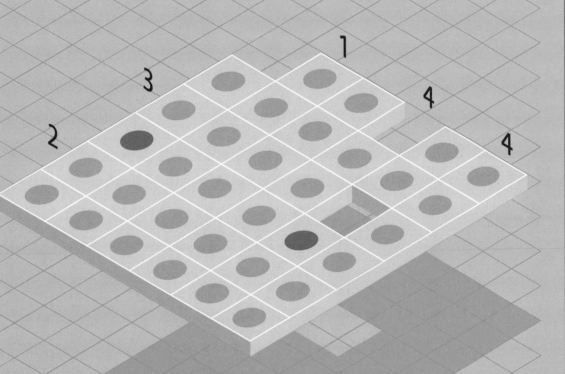

Answer see page 271

16 Place a digit from 1 to 8 into every square, so that each digit appears once in every row and column. Squares separated by a pink peg must contain two consecutive numbers, such as 2 and 3. Squares separated by a red peg must contain numbers where one is twice the value of the other, such as 2 and 4. All possible dots are given, so if there is no dot, then a neighbouring pair can be neither consecutive nor have one be twice the value of the other. Where 1 and 2 are neighbours, either a red peg or a pink peg might be given, but not both.

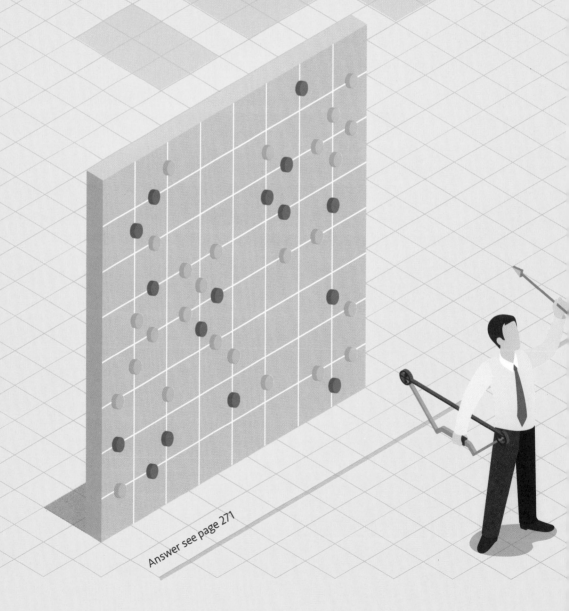

Answer see page 271

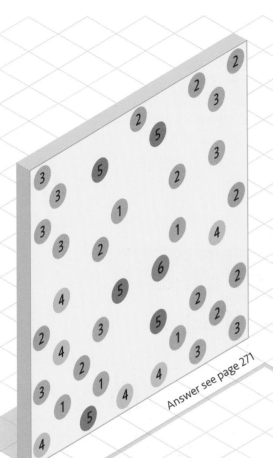

17

Draw horizontal and vertical lines along each row and column of circles to join circled numbers. Each circle contains a number which specifies the number of lines that connect to it. No more than two lines may join any pair of circles. Lines may not cross other lines or circles. All circles must be joined in such a way that you can travel from any circle to any other circle by following one or more lines.

Answer see page 271

18

Can you make each of the totals shown? For each total, choose one number from the outer ring, one number from the middle ring, and one number from the inner ring. The three numbers must add up to the given total.

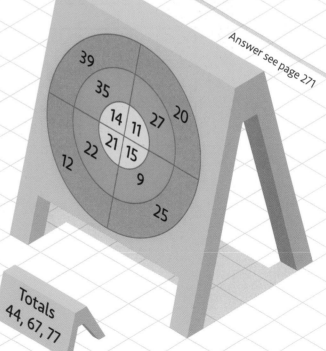

Answer see page 271

Totals
44, 67, 77

19 Place a digit from 1 to 9 into each yellow square, so that no digit repeats in any consecutive horizontal or vertical run of squares. Each horizontal or vertical run has a total given immediately to its left or above, respectively. The digits in that run must add up to the given total.

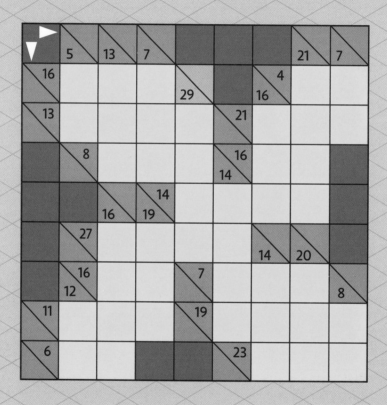

Answer see page 271

20 Reveal a hidden picture by shading some squares, while obeying the clues at the start of each row or column. The clues provide, in reading order, the length of every run of consecutive shaded squares in each row and column. There must be a gap of at least one empty square between each run of shaded squares in the same row or column.

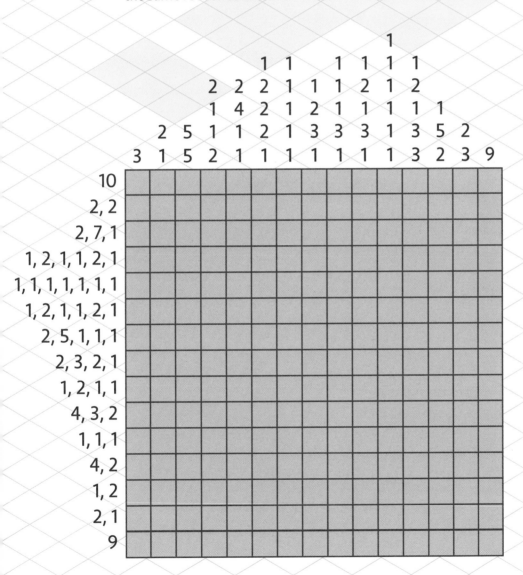

21 Write a number in each empty block so that every block is equal to the sum of the two blocks immediately below it.

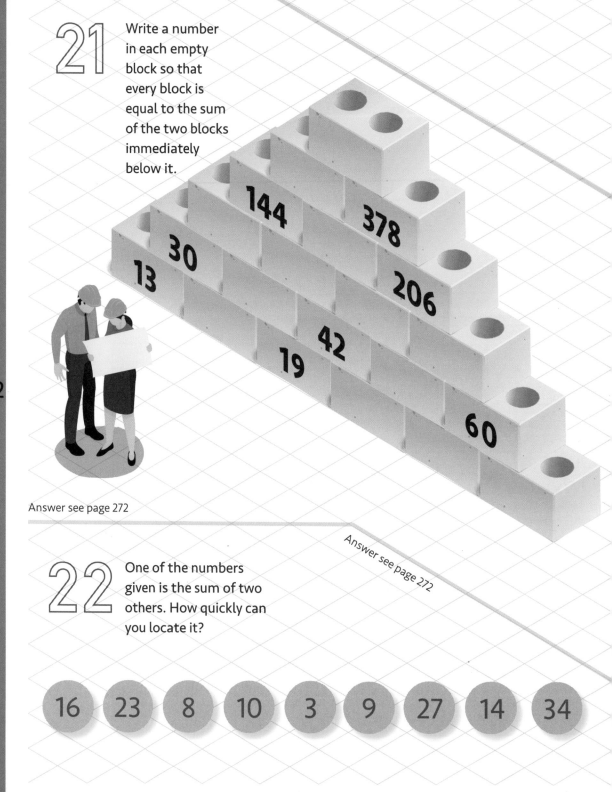

144 378

30 206

13 42

19

60

Answer see page 272

Answer see page 272

22 One of the numbers given is the sum of two others. How quickly can you locate it?

16   23   8   10   3   9   27   14   34

23 Identify the mystery number. Compare the information beside the given numbers. Each digit that appears in the mystery number is marked by a dot. Green indicates a digit in the correct position, red if not. Here, 7152 shares two digits with the mystery number, but only one digit is in the correct position.

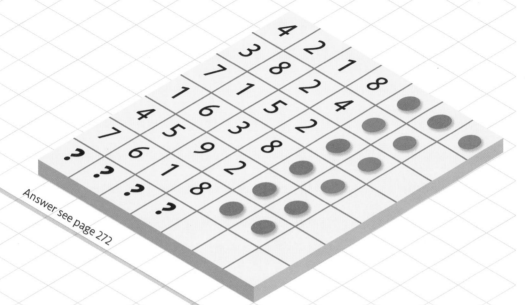

Answer see page 272

24 What is the value of each colour in the grid?

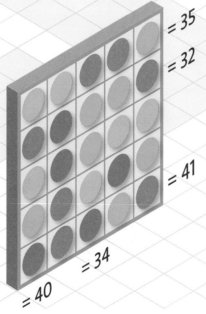

= 35

= 32

= 41

= 34

= 40

Answer see page 272

25 The first two scales shown are balanced. How many triangles are needed to balance the third?

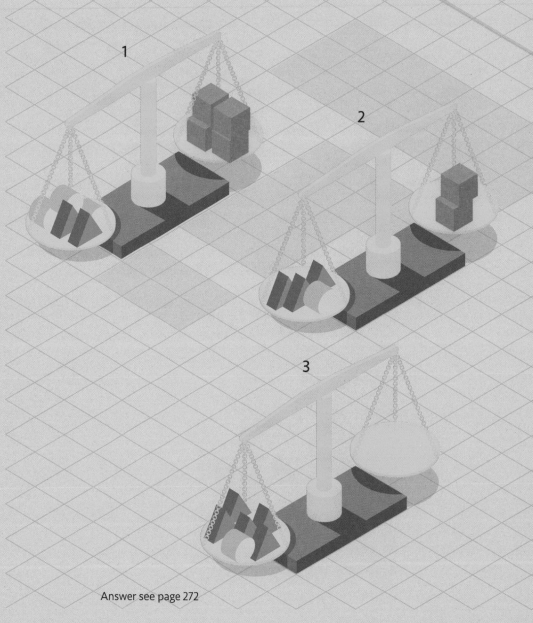

1

2

3

Answer see page 272

26

Each set of numbers represents the name of a male singer, the letters of which have been encoded according to the telephone number pad shown. Who are the singers?

78464
774623
2666
364636
37253
7325
63285623

Answer see page 272

Answer see page 272

27

Fill the grid so that each row and column contains the colours red, green and blue, and two empty squares. The coloured digits surrounding the grid indicate which colour is encountered in which positions along that row or column. For example, a green 1 means the first colour encountered moving from the edge of the grid along the row or column is green, while a blue 2 means the second colour encountered is blue.

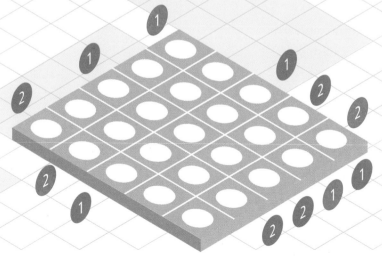

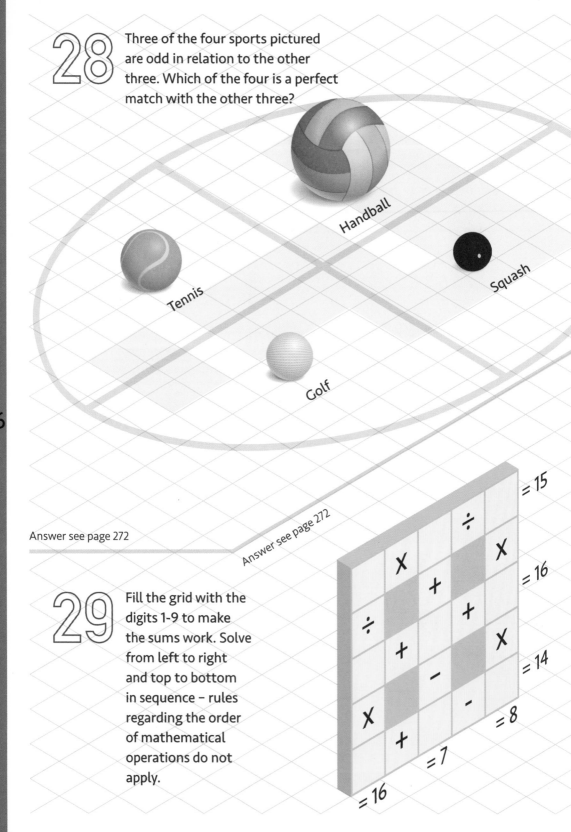

28 Three of the four sports pictured are odd in relation to the other three. Which of the four is a perfect match with the other three?

Handball

Tennis

Squash

Golf

Answer see page 272

Answer see page 272

29 Fill the grid with the digits 1-9 to make the sums work. Solve from left to right and top to bottom in sequence – rules regarding the order of mathematical operations do not apply.

= 15

= 16

= 14

= 8

= 7

= 16

30

What number completes
the sequence?

3   13   1113   3113   132113   ?

Answer see page 272

Answer see page 272

31

Fit the listed
numbers into
the grid.

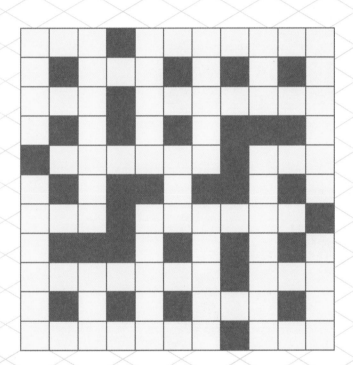

3 digits	745	5 digits	6 digits	7 digits
280	821	31038	349668	5012834
285	834	62038	379608	5109483
291		91524	423615	5702415
345	**4 digits**	91546	473625	6704213
390	2035			6789045
601	2036			9264814
667				
731				

32 Fill in the blank shape following the below rules:

All of the balls have moved position. The top ball is orange, and red is directly above both green and dark blue. The green ball is still not touching the purple ball, which is touching just two other balls.

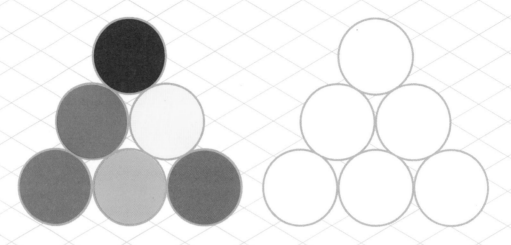

Answer see page 273

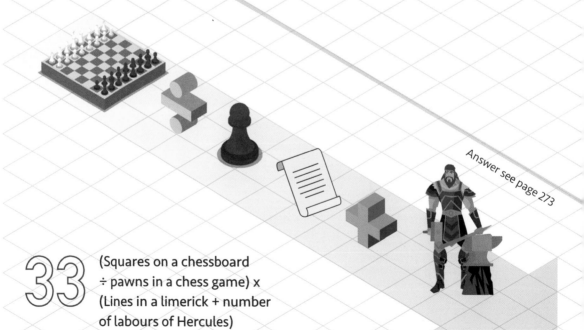

Answer see page 273

33 (Squares on a chessboard ÷ pawns in a chess game) x (Lines in a limerick + number of labours of Hercules)

34 If a sqare sheet of paper is folded along the dotted lines, and cut along the solid lines, which pattern is produced? Note, the cutting is done before folding.

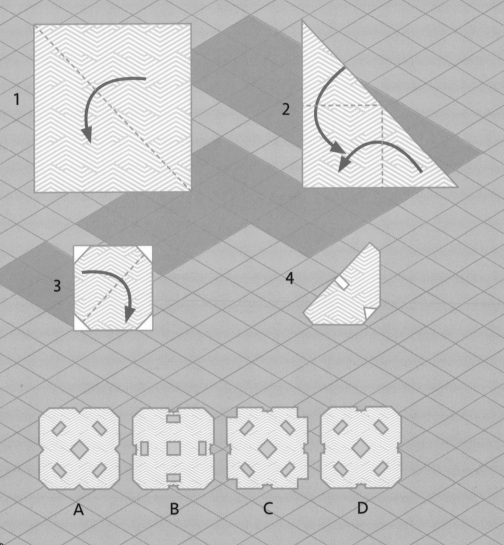

A   B   C   D

Answer see page 273

35

All the answers in this "crossword" are numbers. The unclued answer is a date (month, day, year) of significance in politics.

1	2			3			4		5	6
7				8					9	
10						11	12			
13					14					
	15	16	17						18	
19		20						21	22	
23	24				25					
26			27					28		
29					30					

Across

1 11,111 − 3457
4 $11 \times (9^2 + 10^2)$
7 9 Across reversed + 28 Across
8 $(11 \times 11) + (11 \times 5)$
9 28 Across − 21 Across
10 12 x 139
11 Romans' MMMMDCCLXXIX
13 Last two digits of 6 Down
14 27 x 28
15 UNCLUED
20 Ascending consecutive even numbers
21 Square root of 841
23 4345 − 2387
25 21 Across x 97
26 Centre digits of 10 Across
27 $20^2 - 10^2$
28 20 Across ÷ 9
29 25 Across + 6 Down
30 530 + 631 + 720 + 811

Down

1 22 Down − 1503
2 18 Down − 4 Down − (5 Down + the middle two digits of 23 Across)
3 196 + 222
4 2743 x 6
5 $(27 \text{ Across} \times 3) + 3^3$
6 11 x 127
12 14 Down + 28 Across − 1
14 3 Down + 27 Across
16 21 Across x 5
17 ((20 Across + 100) x 100) + first two digits of 27 Across
18 Anagram of 23 Across, plus a 2
19 A fifth of 20,820
22 1 Across + 10 Across
24 First three digits of 30 Across, reversed
25 A palindrome

Answer see page 273

36

Four runners challenged each other to take part in a marathon. From the information below, work out what fancy dress costume each ran in, the running club they represented, and the time in which they finished.

Dan was dressed as a fairy, while the runner in the pirate costume finished in 3 hours 55 minutes. Annie, not from the Arrows club, finished in a longer time than the runner dressed as a bank manager, who finished in 3 hours 42 minutes. The runner from the Falcons wore the teddy bear outfit. The Cheetah, who wasn't the last to finish in 4 hours 17 minutes, finished two places behind Bakeel. Carly, running for the Jaguars, wasn't the 3 hours 30 minutes finisher.

Answer see page 273

Answer see page 273

37

Fill the 3x3 grid with each of the listed colours as directed: red, orange, yellow, green, blue, purple, pink, brown, black. All references refer to the same row or column, so that "A is above B" means A and B are in the same column, while "C is to the right/left of D" means C and D are in the same row. Pink, which is above blue, is to the left of yellow. Purple, above both red and orange, is to the right of brown. Black is to the right of brown and above green, which is to the right of orange.

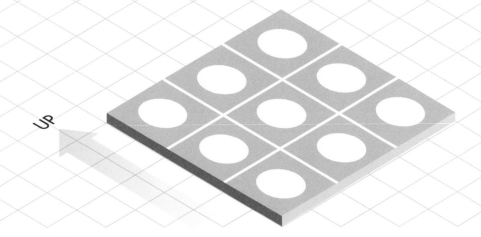

UP

38

A snooty journalist interviewed the winner of the under-18s International Math Tournament. Sunaya, the winner, had enough of his rudeness, so when the journalist asked how old she was, she stumped him. Sunaya told him that if he took her age and multiplied it by two-and-two-thirds her age, he would get 384. How old is Sunaya?

Answer see page 273

39

We've given you two separate equations. Each uses the same digits and each of the mathematical operations +, −, x and ÷. Use each of the given numbers to complete each equation. Solve in sequence from left to right – rules regarding the order of mathematical operations do not apply.

Answer see page 273

4 8 9 36 38

◯ − ◯ x ◯ + ◯ ÷ ◯ = 2

◯ ÷ ◯ x ◯ − ◯ + ◯ = 43

40 Which option most accurately completes the pattern?

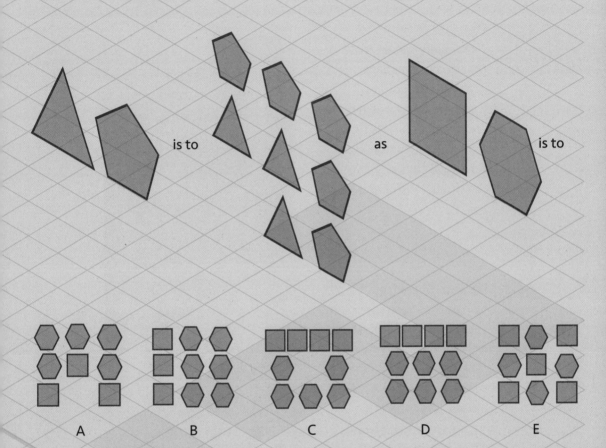

is to ... as ... is to

A   B   C   D   E

Answer see page 273

Test 7

01

Place a digit from 1 to 7 into every square, so that no digit repeats in any row or column. Numbers separated by a greater than or less than sign must obey that sign. Arrows always point to the smaller number of a pair.

Answer see page 273

02

Place numbers from 1 to 9 so that each row, column and bold-lined 3x3 box contains one of each number. Numbers from 1 to 3 must be placed in regular grid squares; numbers from 4 to 6 must be placed in grid squares that contain a green circle; and numbers from 7 to 9 must be placed in grid squares that contain an orange circle.

Answer see page 273

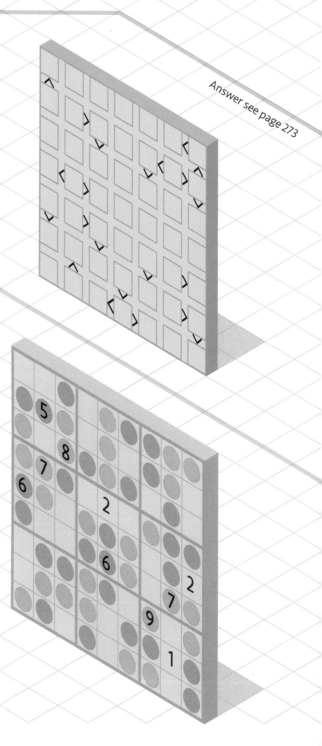

03 Write a number in each empty block so that every block is equal to the sum of the two blocks immediately below it.

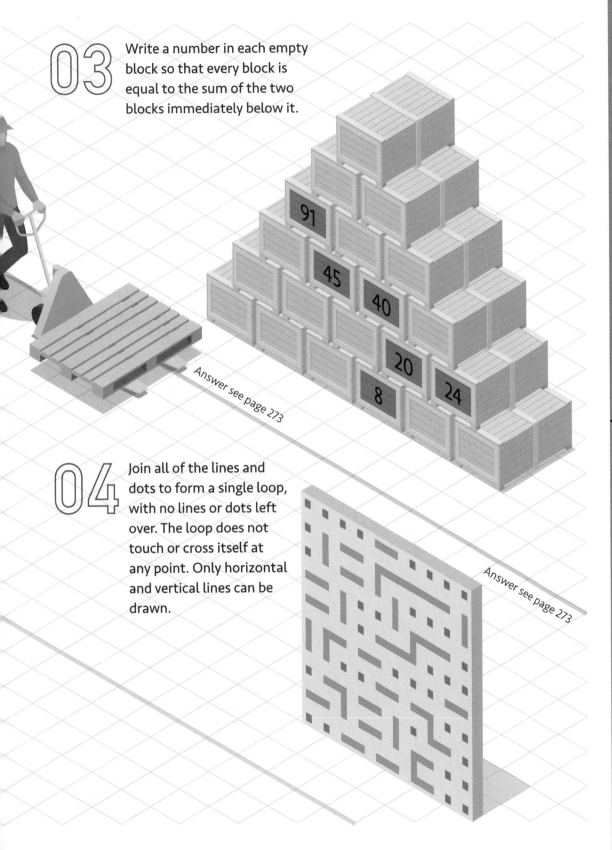

Answer see page 273

04 Join all of the lines and dots to form a single loop, with no lines or dots left over. The loop does not touch or cross itself at any point. Only horizontal and vertical lines can be drawn.

Answer see page 273

Place a number from 1 to 7 once each into every row and column of the grid, while obeying the region clues. The value at the top left of each bold-lined region must be obtained when all of the numbers in that region have the given operation (+, −, ×, ÷) applied between them. For − and ÷ operations, begin with the largest number in the region and then subtract or divide by the other numbers in the region in any order.

05

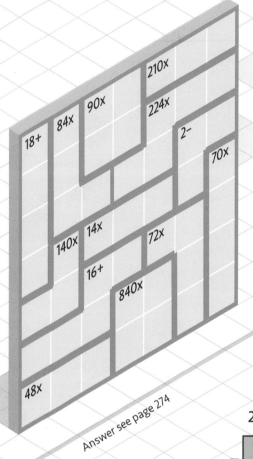

Answer see page 274

Answer see page 274

06

Place a number from 1 to 7 once each in every row and column. Values outside the grid give the total of the numbers in each of the indicated diagonals.

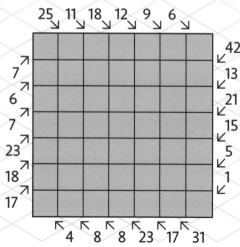

07

Place a colour into each empty square so that every colour appears once in each row, column and bold-lined jigsaw shape.

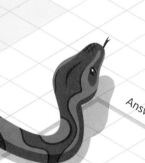

Answer see page 274

08

Shade some squares to form a snake that starts and ends at the snake eyes. Numbers outside the grid specify the number of squares in their row or column that contain part of the snake. A snake is a single path of adjacent shaded squares that does not branch. Shaded squares cannot touch, except for the immediately preceding and following squares in the snake. Shaded squares also cannot touch diagonally, except as necessary for the snake to turn a corner.

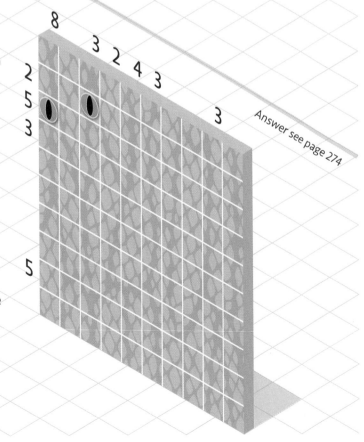

Answer see page 274

Draw a single loop by joining some dots so that each numbered square has the specified number of adjacent line segments. Dots can only be joined by horizontal or vertical lines, and the loop cannot touch, cross or overlap itself in any way.

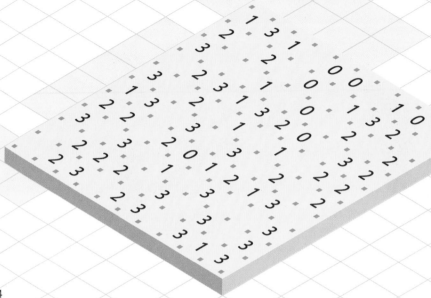

Answer see page 274

Answer see page 274

10

Draw paths to join pairs of matching coloured shapes. Paths can only travel in straight lines between the centres of squares, and no more than one path can enter any square. Paths cannot touch or cross.

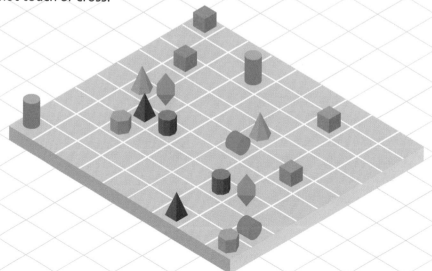

11 Join dots with horizontal and vertical lines to form a single path which does not touch or cross itself at any point. The start and end of the path are given by the red circles. Numbers outside the grid specify the number of dots in their row or column that are visited by the path.

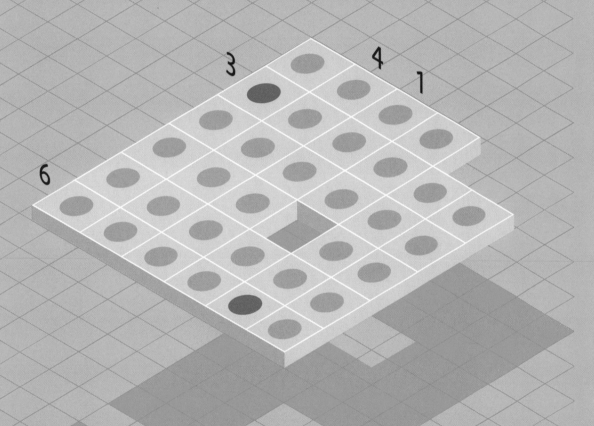

Answer see page 274

12 Place a digit from 1 to 5 into every square, so that no digit repeats in any row or column inside the grid. Place digits in such a way that each given clue number outside the grid represents the number of digits that are "visible" from that point, looking along that clue's row or column. A digit is visible if there is no higher digit preceding it.

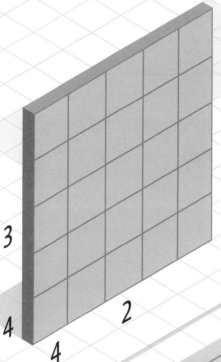

Answer see page 274

13 Place a letter from A to H into every square, so that no letter repeats in any row or column. Identical letters cannot be in diagonally touching squares.

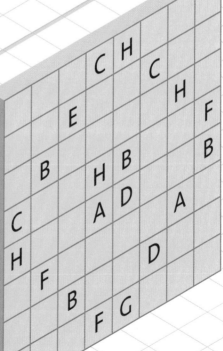

Answer see page 275

14 Draw along the dashed lines to divide the grid to form a complete set of standard dominoes, with exactly one of each domino. A "0" represents a blank on a traditional domino. Use the check-off chart (right) to help you keep track of which dominoes you've placed.

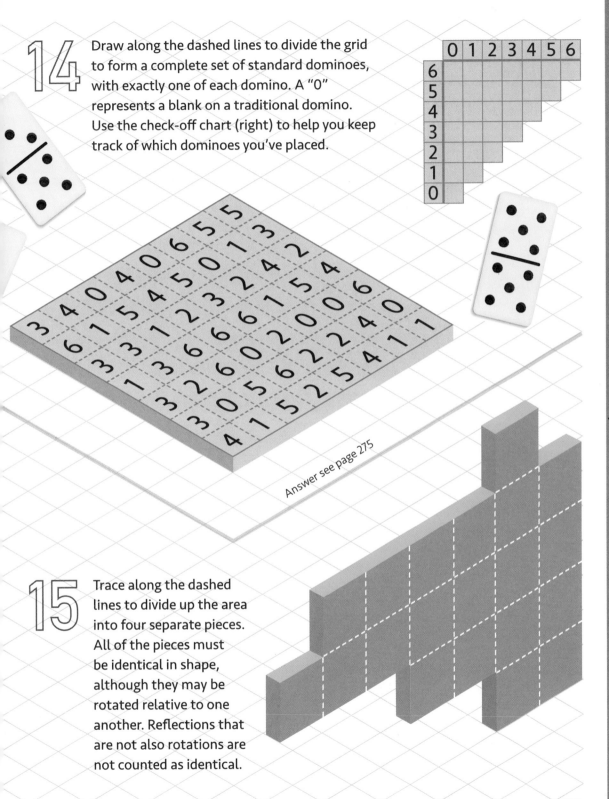

	0	1	2	3	4	5	6
6							
5							
4							
3							
2							
1							
0							

Grid (isometric):
```
3 4 0 4 0 6 5 5 1 3 4 2
6 1 5 4 5 0 3 2 4 1 5 2 4 6
3 3 1 2 3 6 6 1 5 2 0 0
1 3 6 6 0 2 2 2 4 0
3 2 6 0 5 6 2 5 4 1 1
3 3 0 5 2 5
4 4 1 5
```

Answer see page 275

15 Trace along the dashed lines to divide up the area into four separate pieces. All of the pieces must be identical in shape, although they may be rotated relative to one another. Reflections that are not also rotations are not counted as identical.

Answer see page 275

16 Place a digit from 1 to 8 into every square, so that each digit appears once in every row and column. Squares separated by a pink peg must contain two consecutive numbers, such as 2 and 3. Squares separated by a red peg must contain numbers where one is twice the value of the other, such as 2 and 4. All possible dots are given, so if there is no dot, then a neighbouring pair can be neither consecutive nor have one be twice the value of the other. Where 1 and 2 are neighbours, either a red peg or a pink peg might be given, but not both.

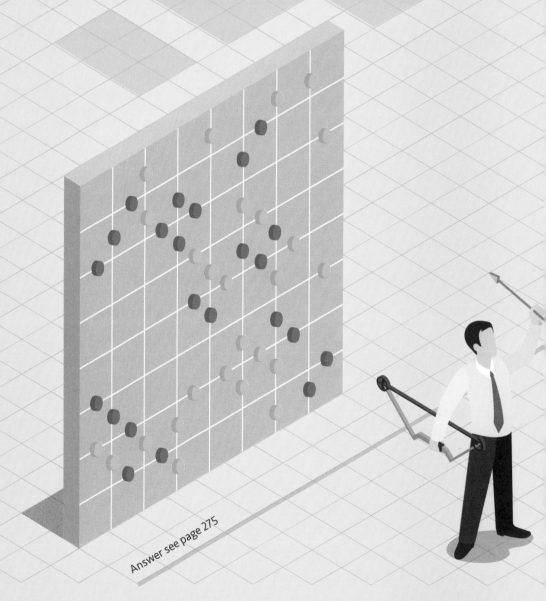

Answer see page 275

17 Draw horizontal and vertical lines along each row and column of circles to join circled numbers. Each circle contains a number which specifies the number of lines that connect to it. No more than two lines may join any pair of circles. Lines may not cross other lines or circles. All circles must be joined in such a way that you can travel from any circle to any other circle by following one or more lines.

Answer see page 275

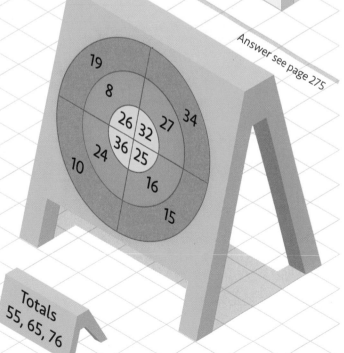

Answer see page 275

18

Can you make each of the totals shown? For each total, choose one number from the outer ring, one number from the middle ring, and one number from the inner ring. The three numbers must add up to the given total.

Totals
55, 65, 76

19 Place a digit from 1 to 9 into each white square, so that no digit repeats in any consecutive horizontal or vertical run of squares. Each horizontal or vertical run has a total given immediately to its left or above respectively. The digits in that run must add up to the given total.

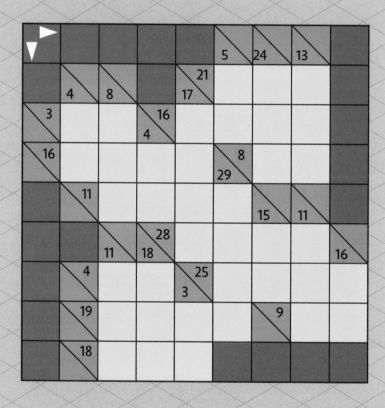

Answer see page 275

Reveal a hidden picture by shading some squares, while obeying the clues at the start of each row or column. The clues provide, in reading order, the length of every run of consecutive shaded squares in each row and column. There must be a gap of at least one empty square between each run of shaded squares in the same row or column.

```
                    2  2  1  3  5  3  1  2  2
                 4  1  2  2  2  2  1  2  1  2  4
              2  5  4  3  1  1  1  1  1  1  1  3  4  5  2
          1
          3
          7
    2, 3, 2
    2, 1, 2
       2, 2
       3, 3
    6, 2, 4
 1, 4, 3, 1
    2, 2, 2
       1, 1
       1, 1
       2, 2
       1, 1
          9
```

21 Write a number in each empty block so that every block is equal to the sum of the two blocks immediately below it.

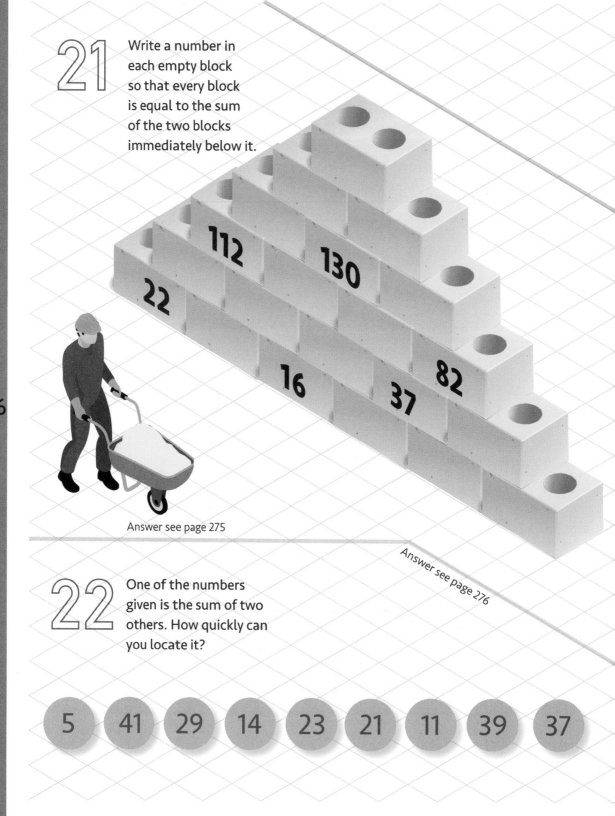

Answer see page 275

Answer see page 276

22 One of the numbers given is the sum of two others. How quickly can you locate it?

5   41   29   14   23   21   11   39   37

23 Fill the grid so that each row and column contains the colours red, green and blue, and two empty squares. The coloured digits surrounding the grid indicate which colour is encountered in which positions along that row or column. For example, a green 1 means the first colour encountered moving from the edge of the grid along the row or column is green, while a blue 2 means the second colour encountered is blue.

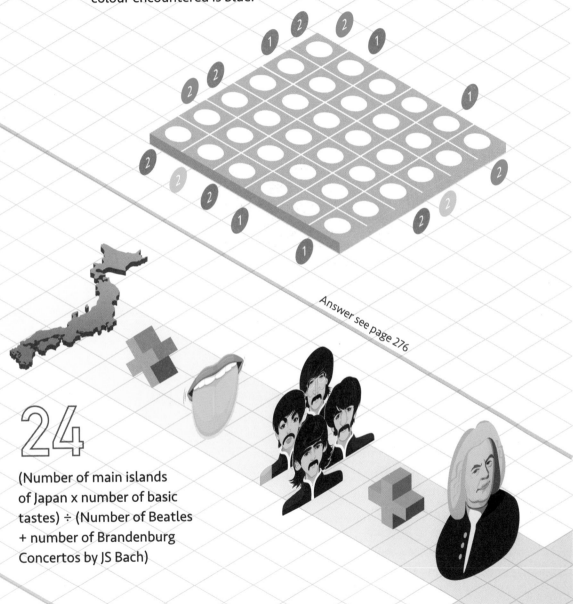

Answer see page 276

24 (Number of main islands of Japan x number of basic tastes) ÷ (Number of Beatles + number of Brandenburg Concertos by JS Bach)

Answer see page 276

25

Three of the four transport options given are odd in relation to the other three. Which of the four is a perfect match with the other three?

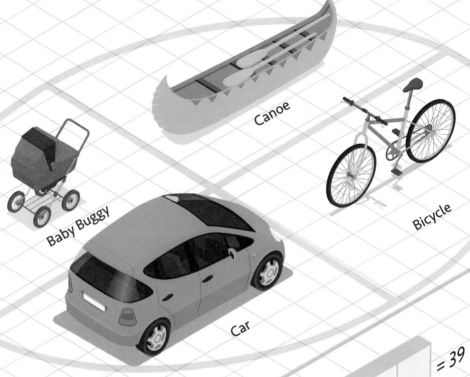

Canoe

Bicycle

Baby Buggy

Car

Answer see page 276

26

Fill the grid with the digits 1-9 to make the sums work. Solve from left to right and top to bottom in sequence – rules regarding the order of mathematical operations do not apply.

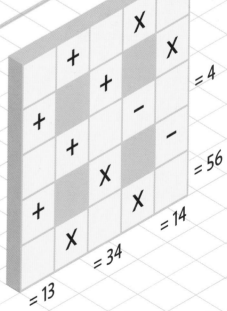

= 39

= 4

= 56

= 14

= 34

= 13

Answer see page 276

27 Fit the listed numbers into the grid.

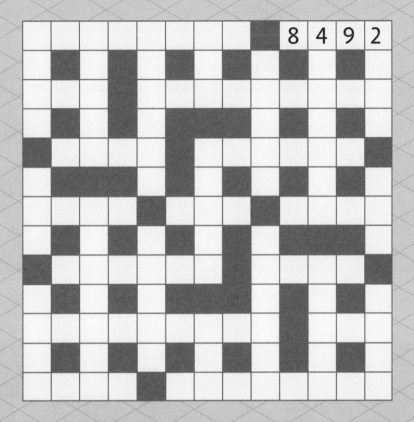

3 digits	4 digits	5 digits	6 digits	8 digits
129	2237	32412	102393	29481350
325	2716	32385	421352	49281530
348	5030	33415	421398	
369	5239	49352	762458	**9 digits**
555	6030	49955		279419304
579	6432		**7 digits**	289620313
738	6519		3422917	
	6830		4530914	
	8492			
	9979			

Answer see page 276

28

Fill in the blank shape following the below rules:

The segments in the outer section stay in the outer section. All but one of the outer segments have changed position, and all of the inner segments have changed position. Green, now opposite yellow and orange, is still in the bottom half of the diagram. Pink, which is still in the top half of the diagram, is opposite purple, which is adjacent to red.

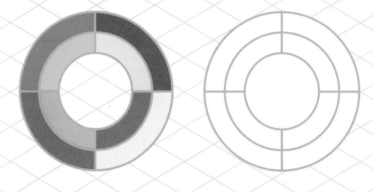

Answer see page 276

29

What is the value of each colour in the grid?

Answer see page 276

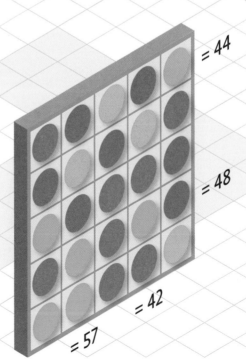

= 44

= 48

= 42

= 57

30 The four images follow a pattern. Which option continues the sequence?

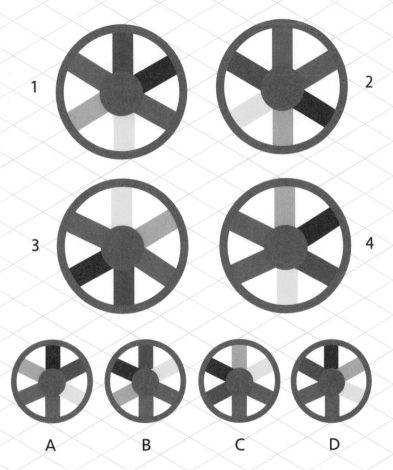

Answer see page 276

Answer see page 276

31 What number completes the sequence?

21 22 44 47 188 193 1158 ?

32

TV's top cooks were each publishing a new cookbook. From the information given, work out the full name of each cook, the cuisine they were focusing on, and the colour of the cover.

Nita's French cookbook didn't have the black cover, nor did the Thai cookbook. The Italian cookbook was written by Schmitt, who wasn't Anna. Fred Russo's book didn't feature the red cover and Dan, who wasn't the cook surnamed MacDonald, went for the blue cover while MacDonald went for the yellow cover. Ms. Patel, who wasn't Anna, didn't produce the vegan cookbook.

Answer see page 276

Answer see page 276

33

We've given you two separate equations. Each uses the same digits and each of the mathematical operations +, −, x and ÷. Use each of the given numbers to complete each equation. Solve in sequence from left to right – rules regarding the order of mathematical operations do not apply.

3 6 8 12 24

◯ − ◯ ÷ ◯ x ◯ + ◯ = 80

◯ ÷ ◯ x ◯ + ◯ − ◯ = 50

34 In the Land of Faerie, pesky pixie Patsy was captured trying to steal the Queen's book of spells. She was brought before Queen Titania who, as judge, jury and executioner, proposed punishment for pesky pixie Patsy. She demanded Patsy make a statement to decide her fate: if the statement were true, Patsy would be banished to Bansheenia, while if the statement were false, she would be exiled to Elfrica. Pesky pixie Patsy's answer made it impossible for her to be banished or exiled. What was her answer?

Answer see page 276

35 The first three scales shown are balanced. How many triangles are needed to balance the fourth?

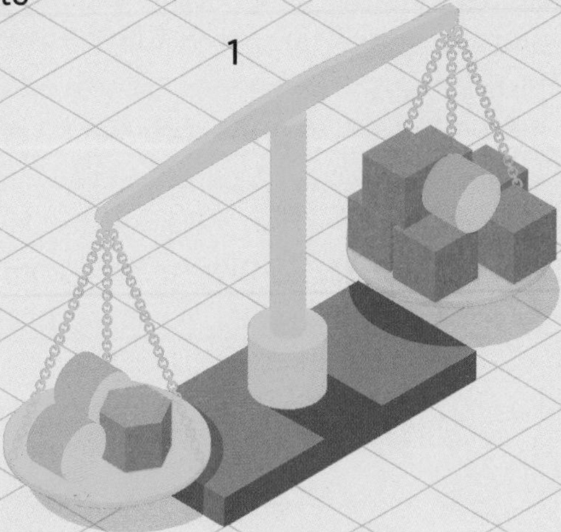

1

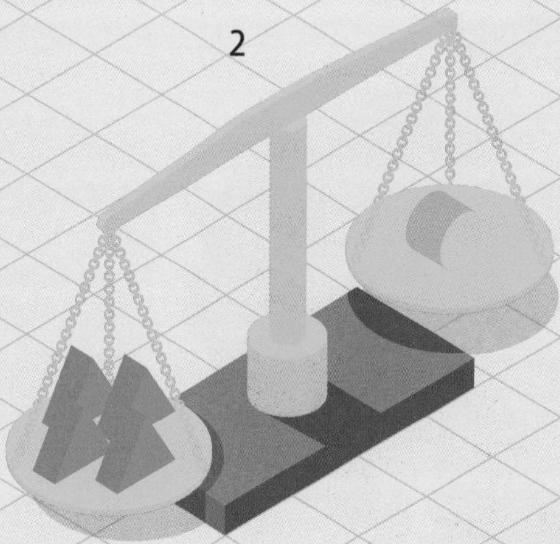

2

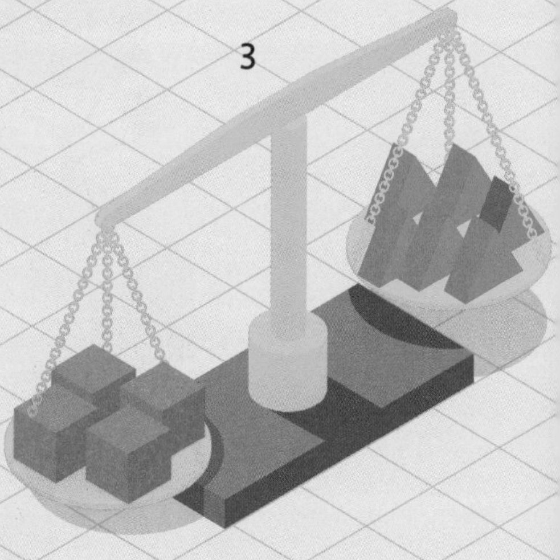

3

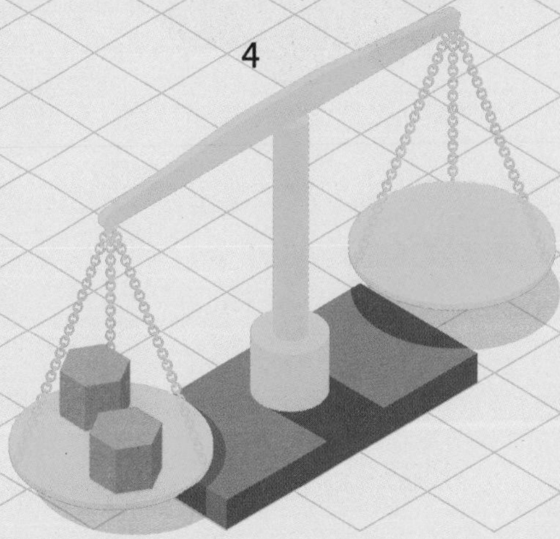

4

Answer see page 276

36

Each set of numbers represents the name of a non-native, English-speaking Oscar-winning actress, the letters of which have been encoded according to the telephone number pad shown. What are the names?

7 3 6 3 5 6 7 3 2 7 8 9
7 6 7 4 4 2 5 6 7 3 6
5 8 5 4 3 8 8 3 2 4 6 6 2 4 3
4 6 4 7 4 3 2 3 7 4 6 2 6
6 2 7 4 6 6 2 6 8 4 5 5 2 7 3

1

2
ABC

3
DEF

4
GHI

5
JKL

6
MNO

7
PQRS

8
TUV

9
WXYZ

0

Answer see page 276

Answer see page 277

175

37

Identify the mystery number. Compare the information beside the given numbers. Each digit that appears in the mystery number is marked by a dot. Green indicates a digit in the correct position, red if not. Here, 2735 shares two digits with the mystery number, but only one digit is in the correct position.

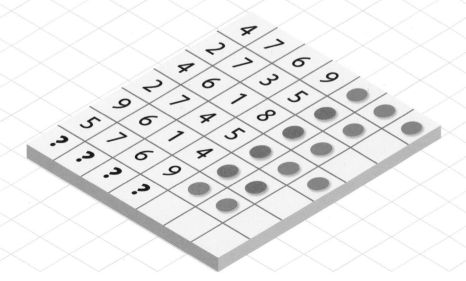

38 All the answers in this "crossword" are numbers. The unclued answer is a date (month, day, year) of significance in transportation.

1	2	3	■	4		5	6	■
7		8		■		9		10
■	11			12		■		
13	14	■	15				16	
■	17	18		■	19			■
20				21		■	22	23
	■	24				25	■	
26	27		■	28			29	
■	30				■	31		

Across

1 22 Across x 27 Down
4 415 + 426 + 436
7 204^2 + 9 Across
9 27 Down x 7
11 8 Down – 12 Down
13 $5^2 + 6^2$
15 4 Across x 52 x 11
17 Ascending consecutive numbers
19 117 x first digit of 8 Down
20 UNCLUED
22 Sum of the first four prime numbers
24 83 x 151
26 Last two digits of 23 Down x 4
28 107 x 109
30 907 x 11
31 133 + 233 + 241

Answer see page 277

Down

1 26 Across x 57
2 Square root of 961
3 16 Down – 29 Down
4 3921 – 1938
5 90,909 – 17,761
6 Half of 26 Across
8 666 x 777
10 Anagram of 17 Across
12 1 Across x 31 Across
14 2 Down x 4
16 10,101 – 9650
18 5 Down – 7 Across
20 One third of 4 Down
21 3169 + 3172 + 3176
23 61 x 117
25 First digit of 20 Down x last two digits of 20 Down
27 7^2
29 Seconds in a minute

39

Which option most accurately completes the pattern?

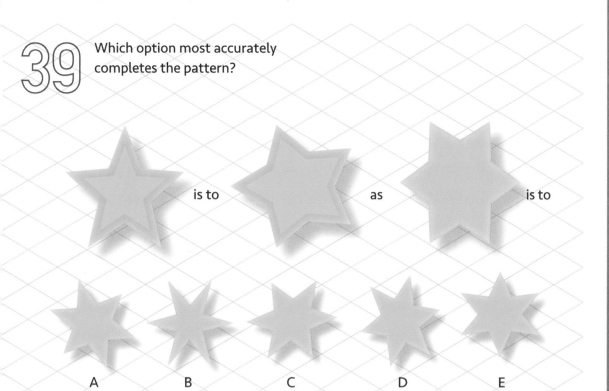

is to   as   is to

A   B   C   D   E

Answer see page 277
Answer see page 277

40

Fill the 3x3 grid with each of the listed colours as directed: red, orange, yellow, green, blue, purple, pink, brown, black. All references refer to the same row or column, so that "A is above B" means A and B are in the same column, while "C is to the right/left of D" means C and D are in the same row. Blue, above yellow and brown, is to the left of pink, and brown is to the left of green. Black is above both green and red, which is to the right of orange. Pink is above purple, which is to the left of green and above orange.

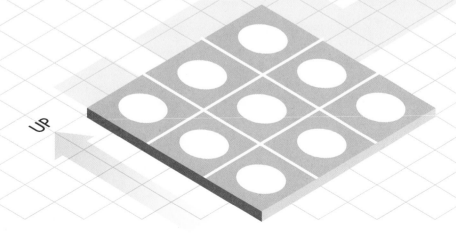

UP

Test 8

01 Place a digit from 1 to 7 into every square, so that no digit repeats in any row or column. Numbers separated by a greater than or less than sign must obey that sign. Arrows always point to the smaller number of a pair.

Answer see page 277

Answer see page 277

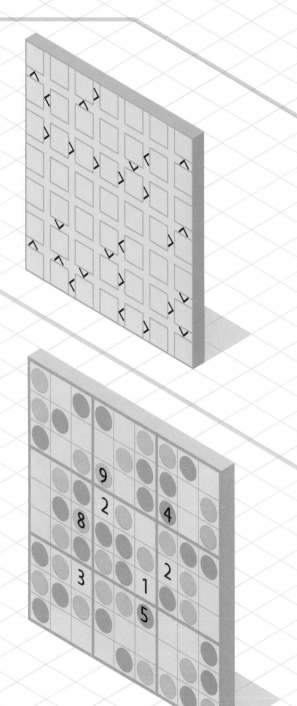

02 Place numbers from 1 to 9 so that each row, column and bold-lined 3x3 box contains one of each number. Numbers from 1 to 3 must be placed in regular grid squares; numbers from 4 to 6 must be placed in grid squares that contain a green circle; and numbers from 7 to 9 must be placed in grid squares that contain an orange circle.

03 Write a number in each empty block so that every block is equal to the sum of the two blocks immediately below it.

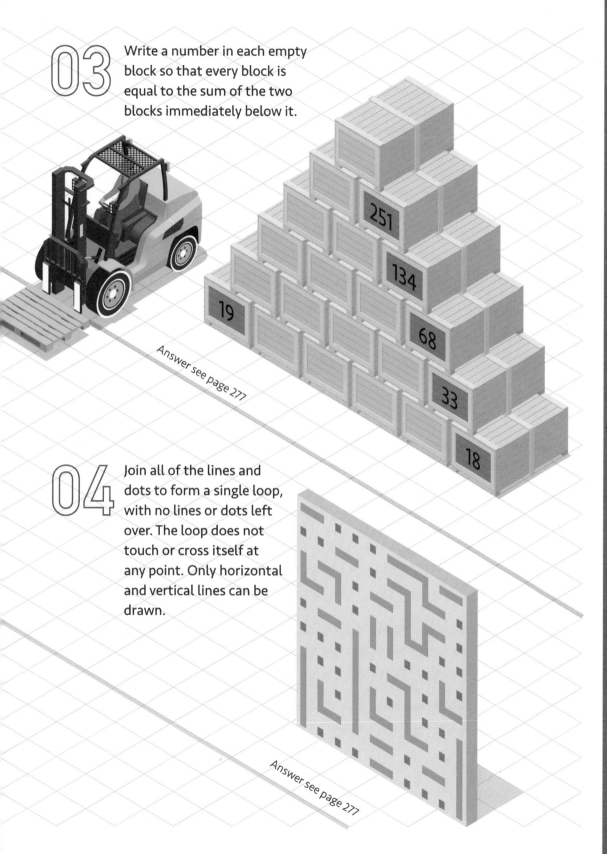

251

134

19

68

33

18

Answer see page 277

04 Join all of the lines and dots to form a single loop, with no lines or dots left over. The loop does not touch or cross itself at any point. Only horizontal and vertical lines can be drawn.

Answer see page 277

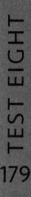

05 Place a digit from 1 to 5 into every square, so that no digit repeats in any row or column inside the grid. Place digits in such a way that each given clue number outside the grid represents the number of digits that are "visible" from that point, looking along that clue's row or column. A digit is visible if there is no higher digit preceding it.

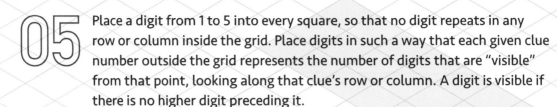

Answer see page 278

06 Place a letter from A to H into every square, so that no letter repeats in any row or column. Identical letters cannot be in diagonally touching squares.

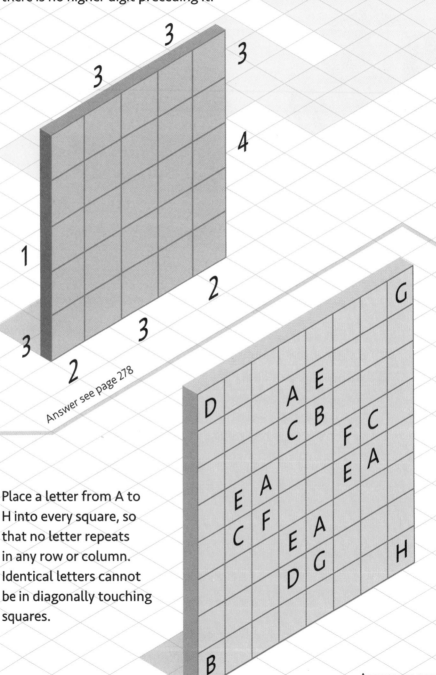

Answer see page 278

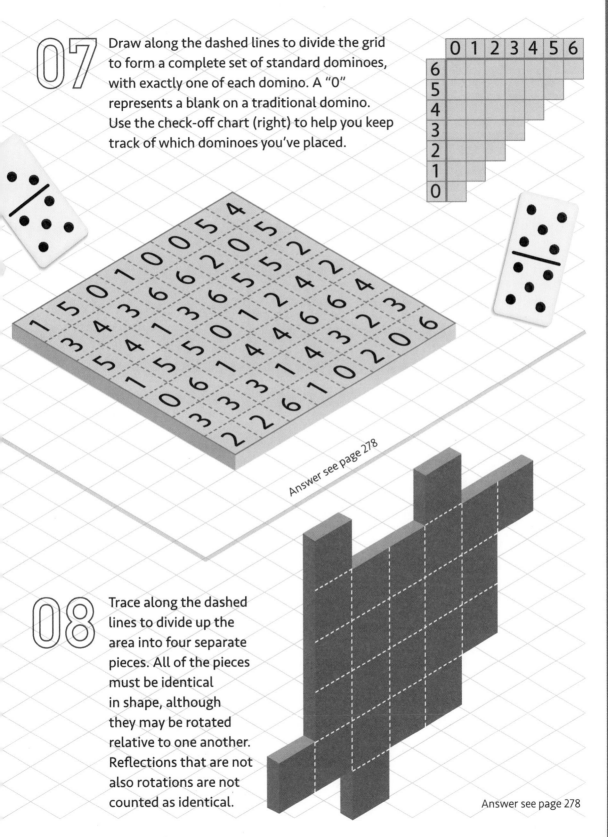

07

Draw along the dashed lines to divide the grid to form a complete set of standard dominoes, with exactly one of each domino. A "0" represents a blank on a traditional domino. Use the check-off chart (right) to help you keep track of which dominoes you've placed.

	0	1	2	3	4	5	6
6							
5							
4							
3							
2							
1							
0							

Answer see page 278

08

Trace along the dashed lines to divide up the area into four separate pieces. All of the pieces must be identical in shape, although they may be rotated relative to one another. Reflections that are not also rotations are not counted as identical.

Answer see page 278

09 Place a number from 1 to 7 once each into every row and column of the grid, while obeying the region clues. The value at the top left of each bold-lined region must be obtained when all of the numbers in that region have the given operation (+, −, ×, ÷) applied between them. For − and ÷ operations, begin with the largest number in the region and then subtract or divide by the other numbers in the region in any order.

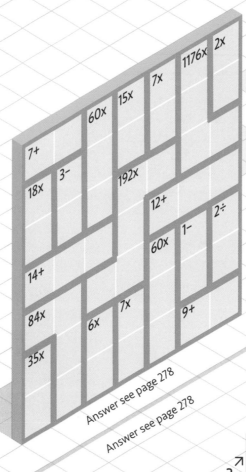

Answer see page 278

Answer see page 278

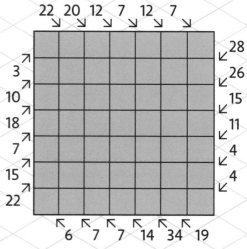

10 Place a number from 1 to 7 once each in every row and column. Values outside the grid give the total of the numbers in each of the indicated diagonals.

11

Place a colour into each empty square so that every colour appears once in each row, column and bold-lined jigsaw shape.

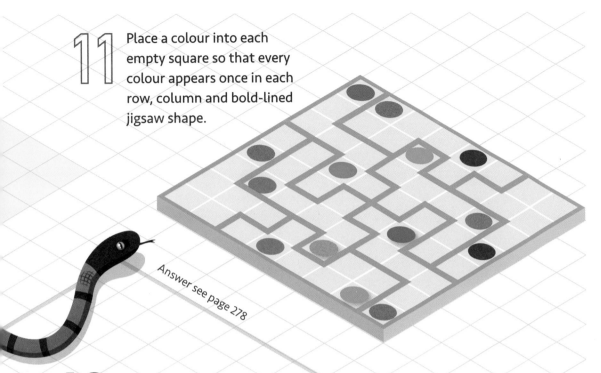

Answer see page 278

12

Shade some squares to form a snake that starts and ends at the snake eyes. Numbers outside the grid specify the number of squares in their row or column that contain part of the snake. A snake is a single path of adjacent shaded squares that does not branch. Shaded squares cannot touch, except for the immediately preceding and following squares in the snake. Shaded squares also cannot touch diagonally, except as necessary for the snake to turn a corner.

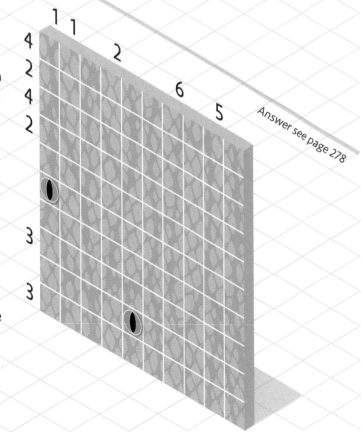

Answer see page 278

13 Draw a single loop by joining some dots so that each numbered square has the specified number of adjacent line segments. Dots can only be joined by horizontal or vertical lines, and the loop cannot touch, cross or overlap itself in any way.

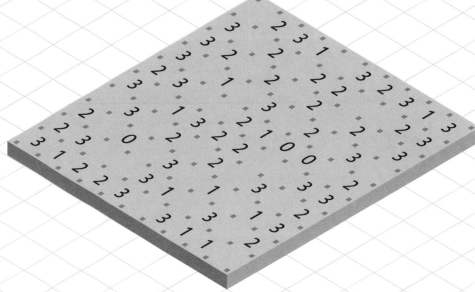

Answer see page 278

14 Draw paths to join pairs of matching coloured shapes. Paths can only travel in straight lines between the centres of squares, and no more than one path can enter any square. Paths cannot touch or cross.

Answer see page 279

15 Join dots with horizontal and vertical lines to form a single path which does not touch or cross itself at any point. The start and end of the path are given by the red circles. Numbers outside the grid specify the number of dots in their row or column that are visited by the path.

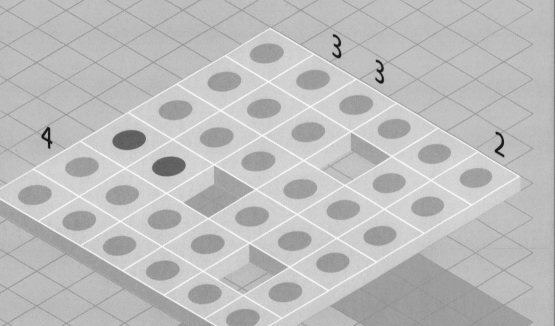

Answer see page 279

16

Place a digit from 1 to 8 into every square, so that each digit appears once in every row and column. Squares separated by a pink peg must contain two consecutive numbers, such as 2 and 3. Squares separated by a red peg must contain numbers where one is twice the value of the other, such as 2 and 4. All possible dots are given, so if there is no dot, then a neighbouring pair can be neither consecutive nor have one be twice the value of the other. Where 1 and 2 are neighbours, either a red peg or a pink peg might be given, but not both.

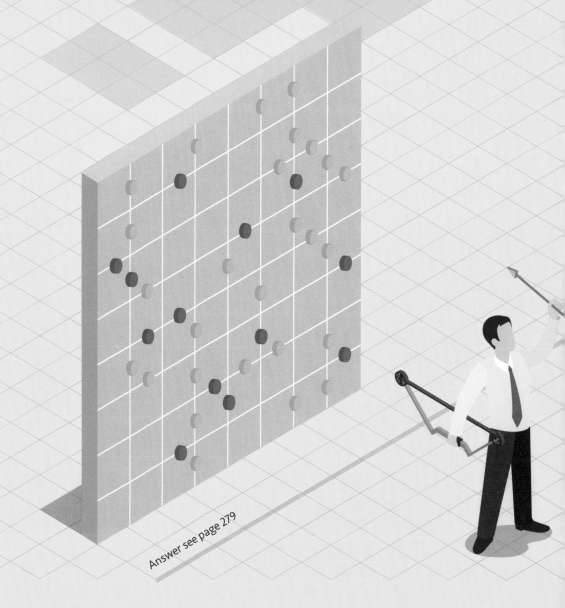

Answer see page 279

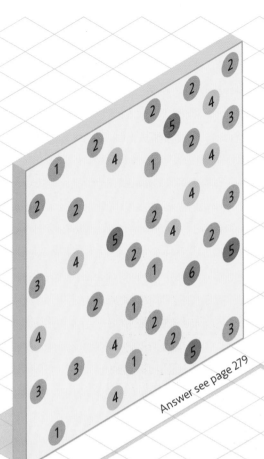

Answer see page 279

17

Draw horizontal and vertical lines along each row and column of circles to join circled numbers. Each circle contains a number which specifies the number of lines that connect to it. No more than two lines may join any pair of circles. Lines may not cross other lines or circles. All circles must be joined in such a way that you can travel from any circle to any other circle by following one or more lines.

18

Can you make each of the totals shown? For each total, choose one number from the outer ring, one number from the middle ring, and one number from the inner ring. The three numbers must add up to the given total.

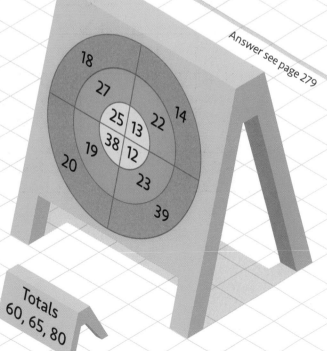

Answer see page 279

Totals
60, 65, 80

19 Place a digit from 1 to 9 into each yellow square, so that no digit repeats in any consecutive horizontal or vertical run of squares. Each horizontal or vertical run has a total given immediately to its left or above, respectively. The digits in that run must add up to the given total.

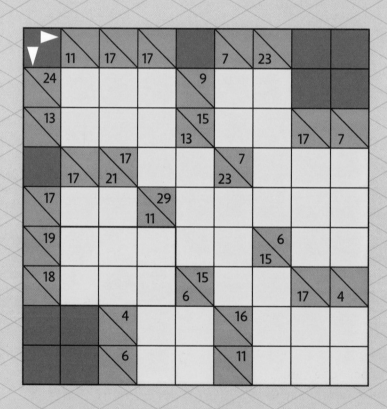

Answer see page 279

Reveal a hidden picture by shading some squares, while obeying the clues at the start of each row or column. The clues provide, in reading order, the length of every run of consecutive shaded squares in each row and column. There must be a gap of at least one empty square between each run of shaded squares in the same row or column.

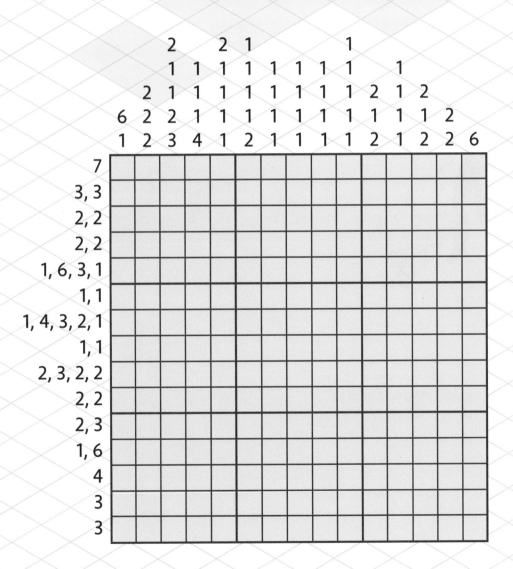

Answer see page 279

21 Write a number in each empty block so that every block is equal to the sum of the two blocks immediately below it.

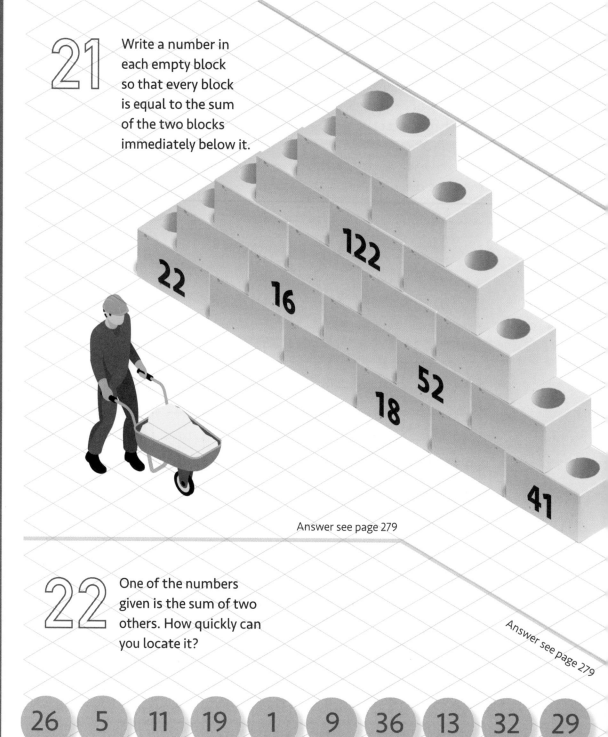

122

22

16

52

18

41

Answer see page 279

22 One of the numbers given is the sum of two others. How quickly can you locate it?

Answer see page 279

26 5 11 19 1 9 36 13 32 29

23

Fill the grid so that each row and column contains the colours red, green and blue, and two empty squares. The coloured digits surrounding the grid indicate which colour is encountered in which positions along that row or column. For example, a green 1 means the first colour encountered moving from the edge of the grid along the row or column is green, while a blue 2 means the second colour encountered is blue.

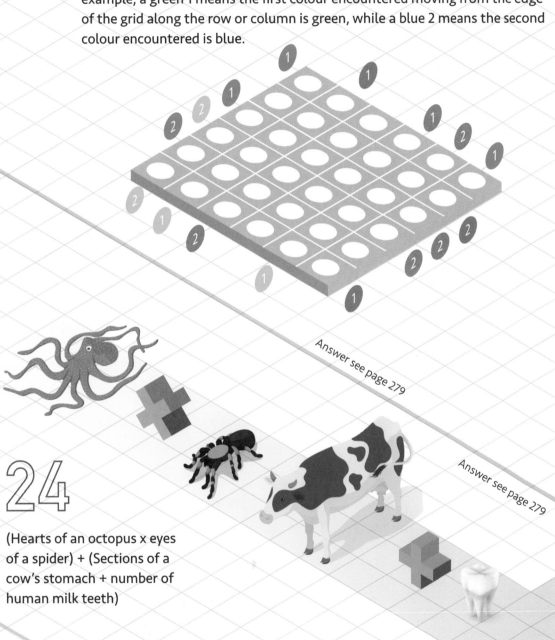

Answer see page 279

24

(Hearts of an octopus x eyes of a spider) + (Sections of a cow's stomach + number of human milk teeth)

Answer see page 279

25 The first three scales shown are balanced. How many hexagons are needed to balance the fourth?

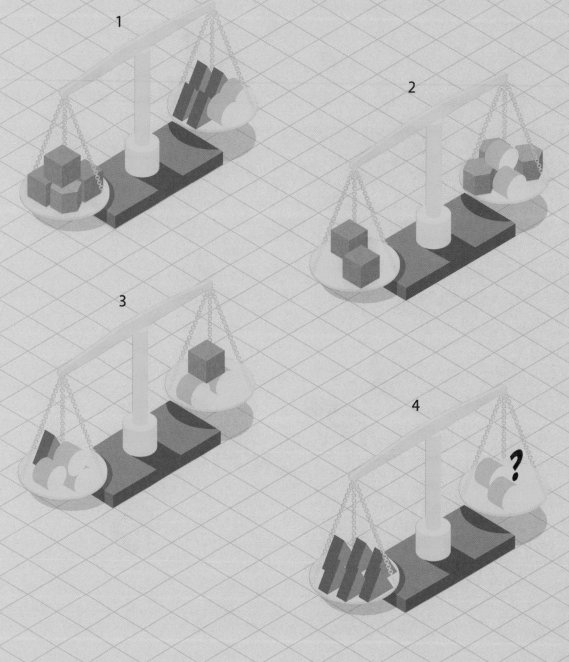

1

2

3

4

?

Answer see page 280

26

Each set of numbers represents the name of a male Shakespeare character, the letters of which have been encoded according to the telephone number pad shown. What are the names?

7 6 6 3 6

4 2 6 5 3 8

6 2 2 2 3 8 4

6 7 5 2 6 3 6

3 2 5 7 8 2 3 3

6 7 7 4 6 6

6 2 5 8 6 5 4 6

Answer see page 280

Answer see page 280

27

Identify the mystery number. Compare the information beside the given numbers. Each digit that appears in the mystery number is marked by a dot. Green indicates a digit in the correct position, red if not. Here, 3579 shares two digits with the mystery number, but only one digit is in the correct position.

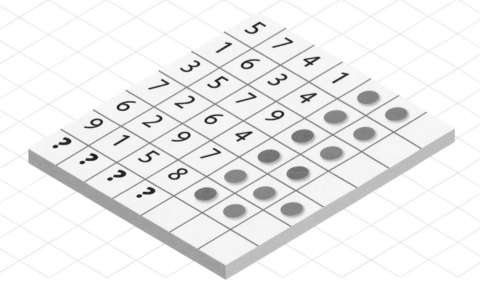

28

Three of the four countries pictured are odd in relation to the other three. Which of the four is a perfect match with the other three?

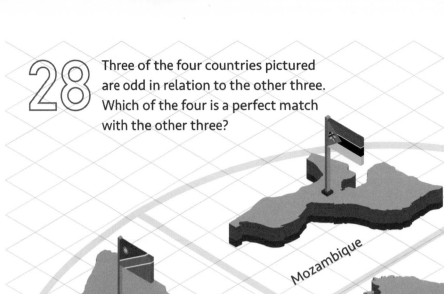

Mozambique

Namibia

Canada

New Zealand

Answer see page 280

Answer see page 280

29

Fill the grid with the digits 1-9 to make the sums work. Solve from left to right and top to bottom in sequence – rules regarding the order of mathematical operations do not apply.

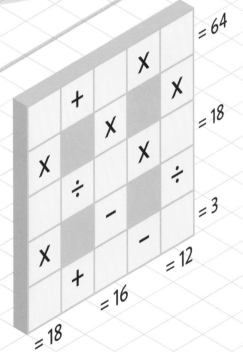

30 Fit the listed numbers into the grid.

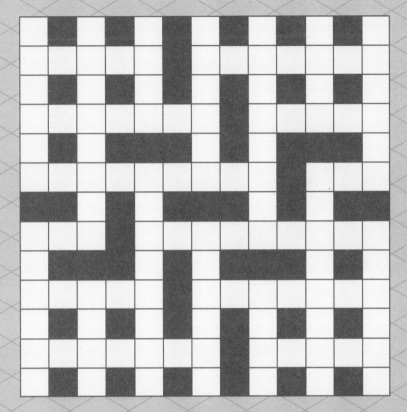

3 digits	**5 digits**	**6 digits**	**7 digits**	**8 digits**
508	31415	137546	1027695	52486578
509	32843	235630	2549823	54138729
	72803	527526	3548383	94123789
4 digits	75723	831534	5188647	98286878
2379		836509		
2396		935734		**9 digits**
8346				178398442
8364				618398447

Answer see page 280

31 Fill in the blank shape following the below rules:

Every diamond has moved. Green and yellow remain in the top half of the grid, while pink is the only diamond to remain in the bottom half. Pink is only adjacent to orange and yellow, the latter of which is also adjacent to blue and purple. Purple is to the right of red.

32 What is the value of orange?

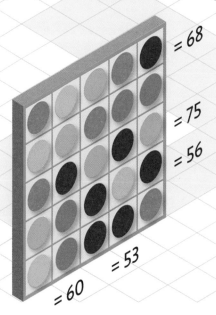

= 68

= 75

= 56

= 53

= 60

Answer see page 280

Answer see page 280

33 If a square sheet of paper is folded along the dotted lines, and cut along the solid lines, which pattern is produced? Note that cutting is done before folding.

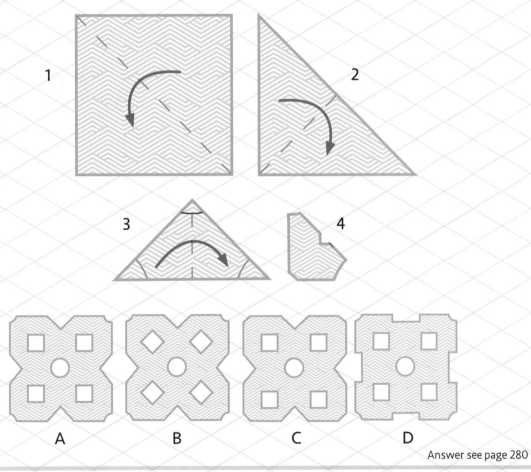

A   B   C   D

Answer see page 280

Answer see page 280

34 What number completes the sequence?

1   2   6   15   31   56   92   ?

35 On the first morning of his vacation, Birdwatcher Bill observed 12 osprey catching 24 fish in just 36 minutes. Later, in the afternoon, Bill noted that 120 fish were caught over 180 minutes. He forgot to count the number of osprey involved. Work out how many osprey caught 120 fish in 180 minutes to help him complete his records.

Answer see page 280

36 We've given you two separate equations. Each uses the same digits and each of the mathematical operations +, −, x and ÷. Use each of the given numbers to complete each equation. Solve in sequence from left to right – rules regarding the order of mathematical operations do not apply.

Answer see page 280

3 4 5 25 100

◯ − ◯ ÷ ◯ + ◯ x ◯ = 72

◯ − ◯ x ◯ ÷ ◯ + ◯ = 75

37

Four comedy Westerns are scheduled for cinema release next year. From the information provided, work out which film has which leading male and female characters, and who is the director.

Alfred Hitchnot's film, which wasn't *Dry River*, didn't feature Billy Goat or Annie Okay, who weren't characters in the same film. Twiggy Alan's film featured Starr Bell, but not opposite either Big Britches or Wild Bill Hiccup, the latter of whom was in *Dry River*. Calamity June appeared in *Forgotten*, which wasn't the film directed by Cameron James. Martin Scores's film wasn't *Low Noon*. *Low Noon* featured Wild Rose, but not Billy Goat. Wire Twerp was the leading male character in *Dances with Cubs*.

Answer see page 280

38

All the answers in this "crossword" are numbers. The unclued answer is a date (month, day, year) of significance in technology.

1	2		3		4	5	6	7
8			9	10				
		11						
12					13	14		15
16	17		18		19			
			20	21				
22		23					24	
25					26			

Across

1 10,001 − 5005 − 3480
4 6 Down − 19 Down
8 Last two digits of 4 Down
9 UNCLUED
11 10,264 ÷ 8
12 262 x 36
13 541 x 22 Down
16 667 + 11 Down + 25 Across
19 13 Across − 4820
20 103 x 8 Across
22 404 x 275
24 4^2
25 212 x 7 Down
26 4 Across + 16 Across

Down

1 15 Down − 22 Across
2 1010 − 954
3 Anagram of 4 Across x 2
4 2 Down squared
5 $2^3 + 3^3 + 4^3$
6 707 x 7
7 First double-digit prime
10 2 Down + 22 Down
11 First two digits of 15 Down x 2 Down
14 678 x 6
15 492 squared
17 Anagram of 18 Down
18 207 x 24 Across
19 2 Down x 24 Down
21 Square root of 4900
22 Half of (7 Down + 23 Down)
23 First two digits of 1 Down
24 Half of 8 Across

Answer see page 280

Which option most accurately completes the pattern?

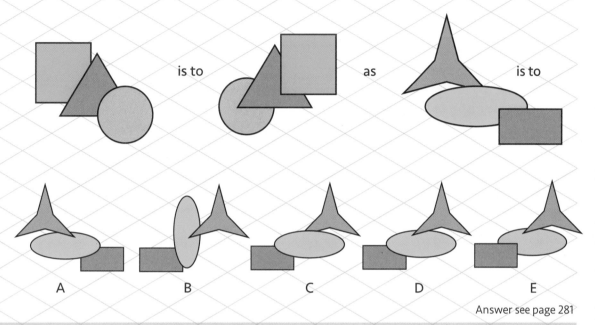

is to ... as ... is to

A   B   C   D   E

Answer see page 281

Answer see page 281

Fill the 3x3 grid with each of the listed colours as directed: red, orange, yellow, green, blue, purple, pink, brown, black. All references refer to the same row or column, so that "A is above B" means A and B are in the same column, while "C is to the right/left of D" means C and D are in the same row. Purple is above red and to the right of orange and brown. Green is above orange. Yellow, to the left of green and blue, is above black. Blue is above purple and red, which is to the right of pink.

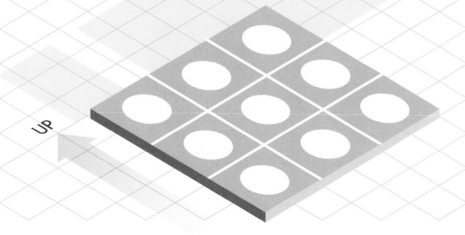

UP

Test 9

01 Place a letter from A to H into every square, so that no letter repeats in any row or column. Identical letters cannot be in diagonally touching squares.

Answer see page 281

	E	D				H	
G	D			C	F	B	
		F	D				
		A			D		
A	F		B	G			
	B		A				
					G	H	
				D			

02 Draw paths to join pairs of matching coloured shapes. Paths can only travel in straight lines between the centres of squares, and no more than one path can enter any square. Paths cannot touch or cross.

Answer see page 281

03 Write a number in each empty block so that every block is equal to the sum of the two blocks immediately below it.

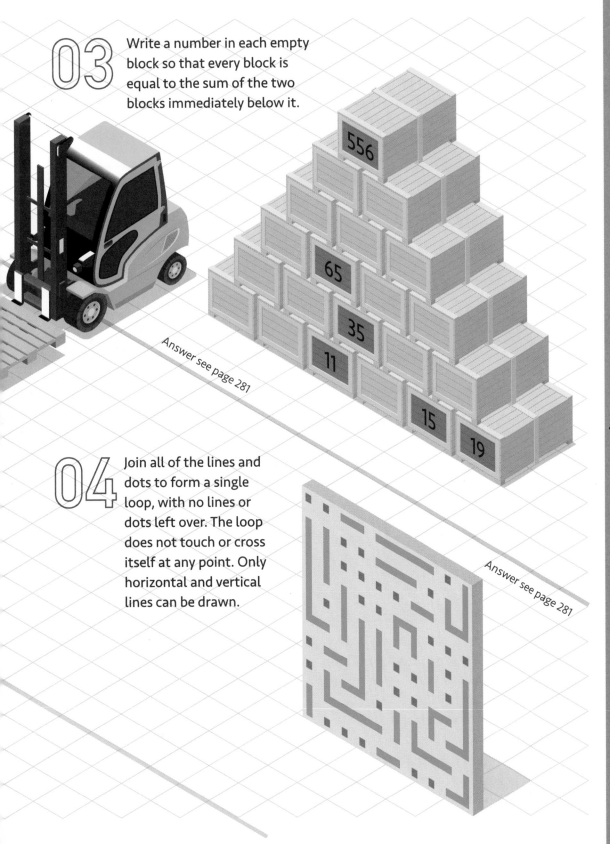

556

65

35

11

15

19

Answer see page 281

04 Join all of the lines and dots to form a single loop, with no lines or dots left over. The loop does not touch or cross itself at any point. Only horizontal and vertical lines can be drawn.

Answer see page 281

05 Place a number from 1 to 8 once each into every row and column of the grid, while obeying the region clues. The value at the top left of each bold-lined region must be obtained when all of the numbers in that region have the given operation (+, −, ×, ÷) applied between them. For − and ÷ operations, begin with the largest number in the region and then subtract or divide by the other numbers in the region in any order.

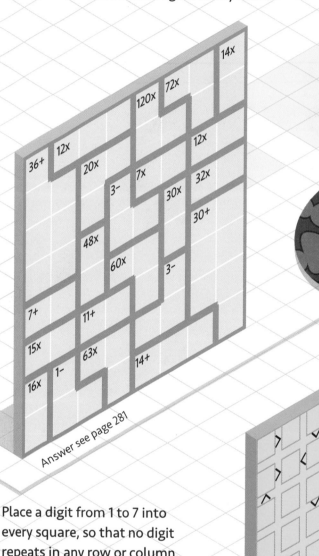

Answer see page 281

06 Place a digit from 1 to 7 into every square, so that no digit repeats in any row or column. Numbers separated by a greater than or less than sign must obey that sign. Arrows always point to the smaller number of a pair.

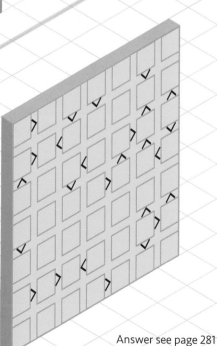

Answer see page 281

Place a colour into each empty square so that every colour appears once in each row, column and bold-lined jigsaw shape.

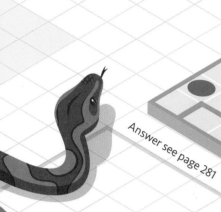

Answer see page 281

Shade some squares to form a snake that starts and ends at the snake eyes. Numbers outside the grid specify the number of squares in their row or column that contain part of the snake. A snake is a single path of adjacent shaded squares that does not branch. Shaded squares cannot touch, except for the immediately preceding and following squares in the snake. Shaded squares also cannot touch diagonally, except as necessary for the snake to turn a corner.

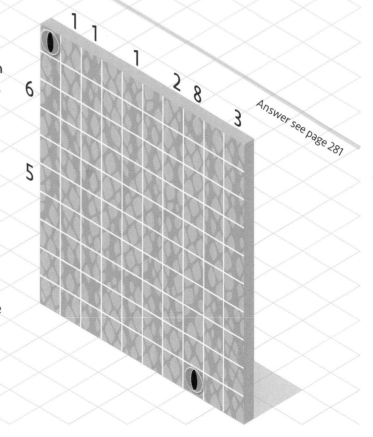

Answer see page 281

09 Place numbers from 1 to 9 so that each row, column and bold-lined 3x3 box contains one of each number. Numbers from 1 to 3 must be placed in regular grid squares; numbers from 4 to 6 must be placed in grid squares that contain a green circle; and numbers from 7 to 9 must be placed in grid squares that contain an orange circle.

Answer see page 282

10 Draw a single loop by joining some dots so that each numbered square has the specified number of adjacent line segments. Dots can only be joined by horizontal or vertical lines, and the loop cannot touch, cross or overlap itself in any way.

Answer see page 282

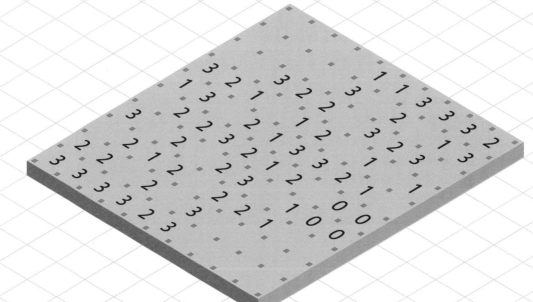

11 Join dots with horizontal and vertical lines to form a single path which does not touch or cross itself at any point. The start and end of the path are given by the red circles. Numbers outside the grid specify the number of dots in their row or column that are visited by the path.

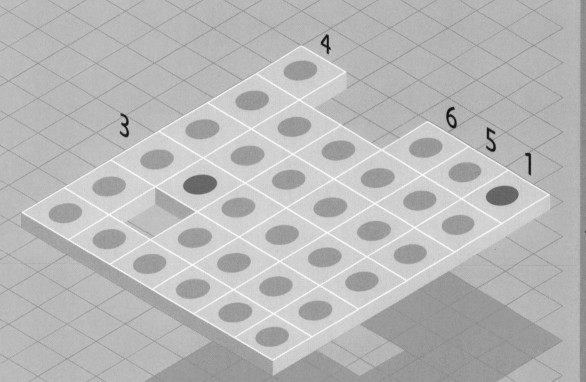

Answer see page 282

12 Place a digit from 1 to 5 into every square, so that no digit repeats in any row or column inside the grid. Place digits in such a way that each given clue number outside the grid represents the number of digits that are "visible" from that point, looking along that clue's row or column. A digit is visible if there is no higher digit preceding it.

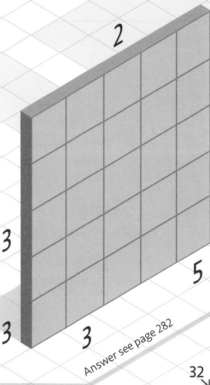

2

3

5

3   3

Answer see page 282

13 Place a number from 1 to 7 once each in every row and column. Values outside the grid give the total of the numbers in each of the indicated diagonals.

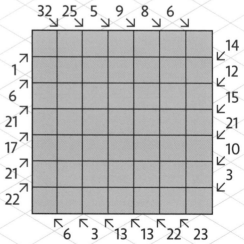

32 25 5 9 8 6

1
6
21
17
21
22

14
12
15
21
10
3

6 3 13 13 22 23

Answer see page 282

14 Draw along the dashed lines to divide the grid to form a complete set of standard dominoes, with exactly one of each domino. A "0" represents a blank on a traditional domino. Use the check-off chart (right) to help you keep track of which dominoes you've placed.

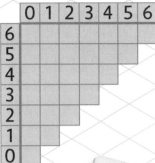

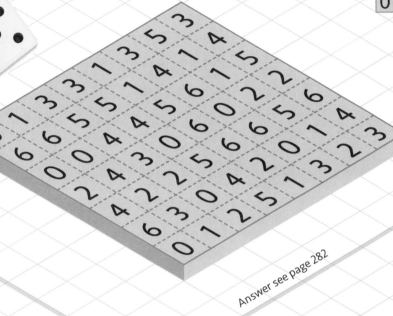

Answer see page 282

15 Trace along the dashed lines to divide up the area into four separate pieces. All of the pieces must be identical in shape, although they may be rotated relative to one another. Reflections that are not also rotations are not counted as identical.

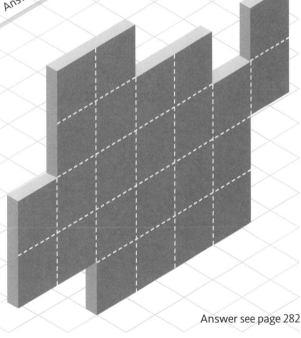

Answer see page 282

16

Place a digit from 1 to 8 into every square, so that each digit appears once in every row and column. Squares separated by a pink peg must contain two consecutive numbers, such as 2 and 3. Squares separated by a red peg must contain numbers where one is twice the value of the other, such as 2 and 4. All possible dots are given, so if there is no dot, then a neighbouring pair can be neither consecutive nor have one be twice the value of the other. Where 1 and 2 are neighbours, either a red peg or a pink peg might be given, but not both.

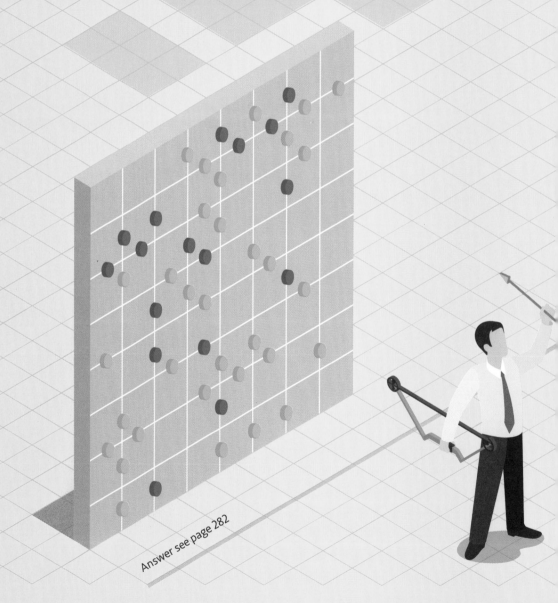

Answer see page 282

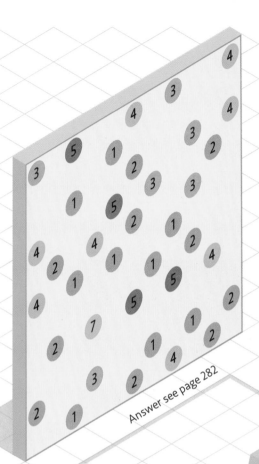

17 Draw horizontal and vertical lines along each row and column of circles to join circled numbers. Each circle contains a number which specifies the number of lines that connect to it. No more than two lines may join any pair of circles. Lines may not cross other lines or circles. All circles must be joined in such a way that you can travel from any circle to any other circle by following one or more lines.

Answer see page 282

18 Can you make each of the totals shown? For each total, choose one number from the outer ring, one number from the middle ring, and one number from the inner ring. The three numbers must add up to the given total.

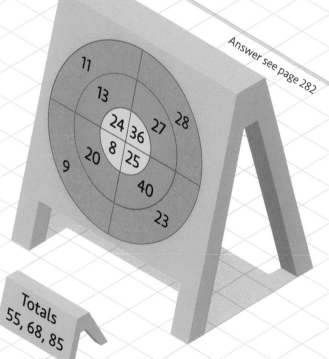

Answer see page 282

Totals
55, 68, 85

19

Place a digit from 1 to 9 into each yellow square, so that no digit repeats in any consecutive horizontal or vertical run of squares. Each horizontal or vertical run has a total given immediately to its left or above, respectively. The digits in that run must add up to the given total.

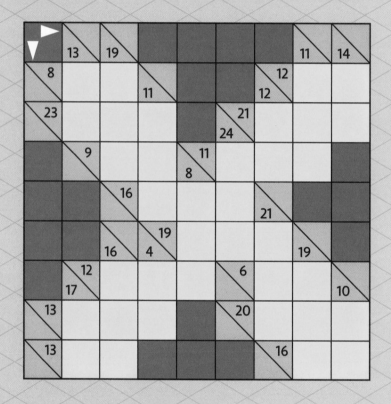

Answer see page 283

20 Reveal a hidden picture by shading some squares, while obeying the clues at the start of each row or column. The clues provide, in reading order, the length of every run of consecutive shaded squares in each row and column. There must be a gap of at least one empty square between each run of shaded squares in the same row or column.

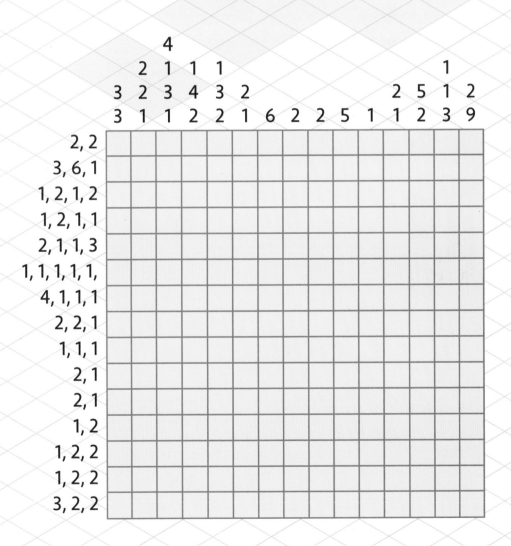

Answer see page 283

21 Write a number in each empty block so that every block is equal to the sum of the two blocks immediately below it.

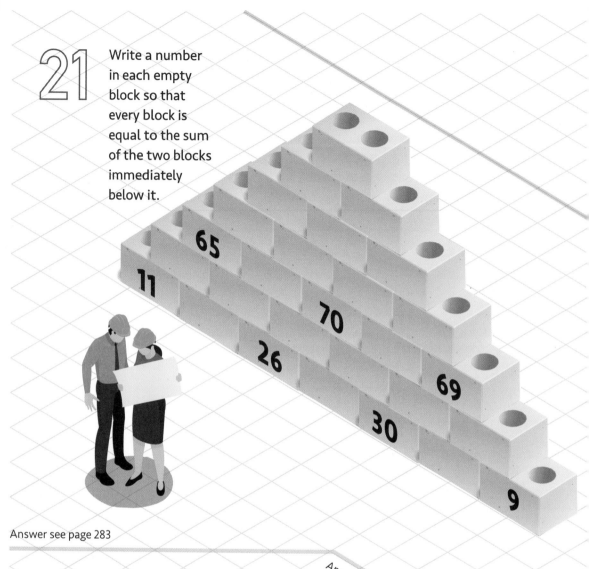

65

11

70

26

69

30

9

Answer see page 283

22 One of the numbers given is the sum of two others. How quickly can you locate it?

Answer see page 283

32   25   4   12   26   9   27   19   17

23 Identify the mystery number. Compare the information beside the given numbers. Each digit that appears in the mystery number is marked by a dot. Green indicates a digit in the correct position, red if not. Here, 8165 shares two digits with the mystery number, but only one digit is in the correct position.

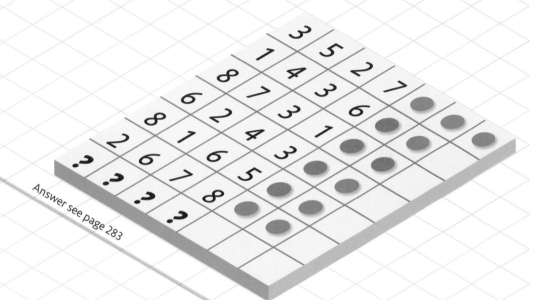

Answer see page 283

24 My grandfather was 69 when I was 13. He is now three times as old as I am. How old are we now?

Answer see page 283

25 Three of the four animals pictured are odd in relation to the other three. Which of the four is a perfect match with the other three?

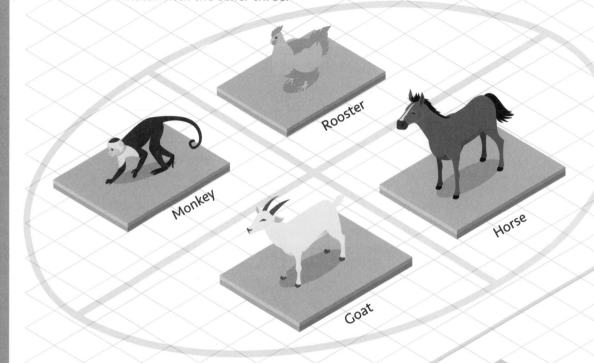

Rooster

Monkey

Horse

Goat

Answer see page 283

Answer see page 283

26 Fill the grid with the digits 1-9 to make the sums work. Solve from left to right and top to bottom in sequence – rules regarding the order of mathematical operations do not apply.

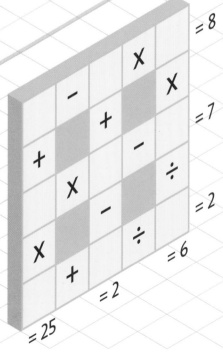

Fit the listed numbers into the grid.

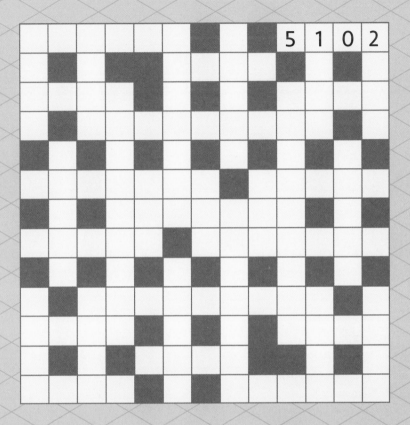

3 digits	2914	**5 digits**	**6 digits**	**9 digits**
243	2915	26543	174262	326498572
244	2945	34851	654432	326698471
342	3314	36154		491375326
	3806	36963	**7 digits**	496715326
4 digits	3986	54092	1494749	
1358	4360	76352	2438756	
1936	4904		2493719	
1943	5102		2637213	
1984	8204		7498756	
2362	8260			

Answer see page 283

28

All the answers in this "crossword" are numbers. The unclued answer is a date (month, day, year) of significance in communications.

1		2	3		4	5		6
		7		8				
9	10					11	12	
13			14		15			
	16	17						
18						19	20	
21					22			
		23	24		25			
26				27				

Across

1   101 x 13 Across
4   1 Across + 4 Down
7   1 Down x 8
9   First two digits of 23 Across x first two digits of 22 Across
11 Descending even numbers
13 Square root of 441
14 19,333 x 3 Down
16 UNCLUED
18 14 Across – 7 Across – 23 Across
19 $4^2 + 5^2 + 6$
21 366 + 9 Across
22 44 + 67
23 21 Across x 19 Across
26 50,725 ÷ 4 Down
27 419×2^4

Down

1   Romans' MMCMXXXII
2   2925 ÷ 13
3   Consecutive ascending odd numbers
4   5^2
5   9523 + 7315
6   $80^2 + 7^2 + 100$
8   7 Across x 22 Down
10 5413 x 15
12 10 Down – 19,054
14 The first 2 digits of 4 Across x 5
15 $4^2 + 7^2 + 11^2$
17 44 x 503
18 134 x 3 Down
20 Anagram of 18 Down
22 24 Down x 3
24 6 Down ÷ 22 Across
25 (2 Down – 22 Down) x 2

Answer see page 283

29

Triplets Tom, Dick and Harry had found love. They each decided to take their partner away to propose. From the information given, work out which triplet proposed to which partner, the metal used for their engagement ring and where it was hidden, where they went for the weekend, and what residence they stayed in.

Paula found a ring made of yellow gold, but not in the coffee pot. The cottage, which wasn't where Fatima was staying, was in Snowdonia. Harry, who wasn't the triplet who proposed in the Lake District, didn't hide his platinum ring in the box of chocolates. The ring hidden in a bunch of flowers was found in the Lake District, though not by Maria, who wasn't staying in the hostel. Tom's trip involved staying in the tent, but not in the Peak District, and his ring wasn't made of white gold. Maria didn't find her ring in the box of chocolates.

Answer see page 284

Answer see page 284

30

Fill the 3x3 grid with each of the listed colours as directed: red, orange, yellow, green, blue, purple, pink, brown, black. All references refer to the same row or column, so that "A is above B" means A and B are in the same column, while "C is to the right/left of D" means C and D are in the same row. Pink is above purple, which is to the right of black and orange. Green is above yellow and to the left of red. Red and orange are above brown, which is to the left of blue.

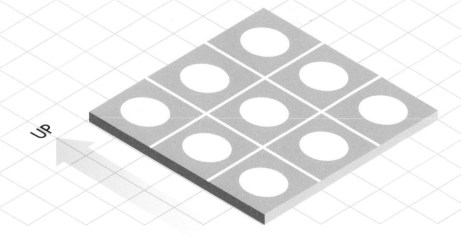

UP

31 Fill in the blank shape following the below rules:

All but one petal on the flower has moved location. The orange petal is now opposite its original position, and next to both the pink and blue petals. The purple petal is between the red and yellow petals.

Answer see page 284

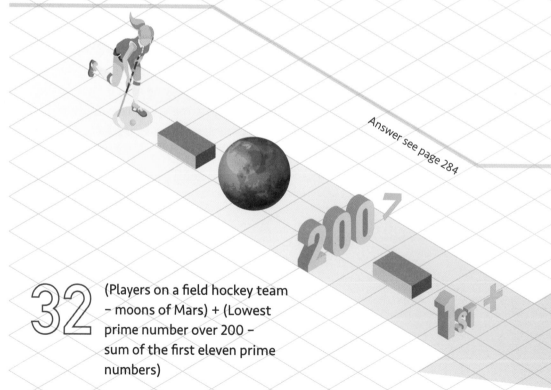

Answer see page 284

32 (Players on a field hockey team – moons of Mars) + (Lowest prime number over 200 – sum of the first eleven prime numbers)

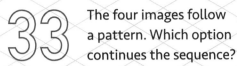

33 The four images follow a pattern. Which option continues the sequence?

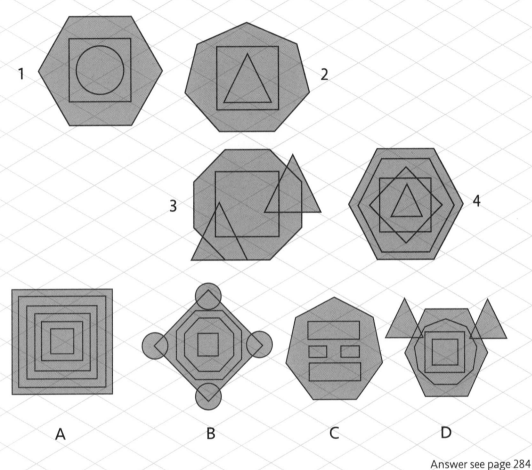

1

2

3

4

A   B   C   D

Answer see page 284

Answer see page 284

34 What number completes the sequence?

2   10   30   68   130   222   350   ?

35 What is the value of each colour in the grid?

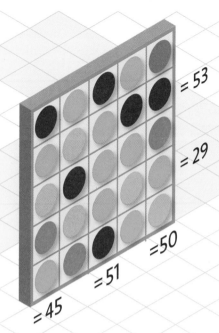

= 53

= 29

=50

= 51

= 45

Answer see page 284

36 We've given you two separate equations. Each uses the same digits and each of the mathematical operations +, −, x and ÷. Use each of the given numbers to complete each equation. Solve in sequence from left to right – rules regarding the order of mathematical operations do not apply.

Answer see page 284

5 6 9 11 12

◯ − ◯ + ◯ ÷ ◯ x ◯ = 12

◯ − ◯ x ◯ ÷ ◯ + ◯ = 12

37

Which option most accurately completes the pattern?

 is to  as  is to

A

B

C

D

E

TEST NINE

223

Answer see page 284

38 The first two scales shown are balanced. How many triangles are needed to balance the third?

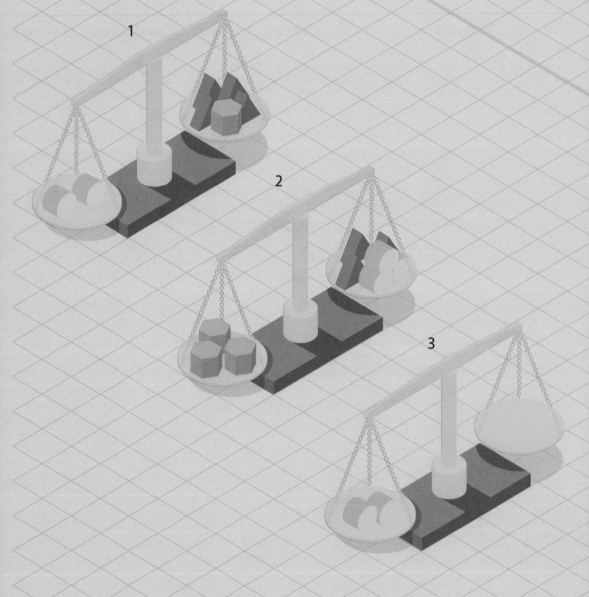

1

2

3

Answer see page 284

Each set of numbers represents the name of a Disney title character, the letters of which have been encoded according to the telephone number pad shown. What are the names?

22624
38626
746622446
73837726
7622466827
68526

Answer see page 284

Fill the grid so that each row and column contains the colours red, green and blue, and two empty squares. The coloured digits surrounding the grid indicate which colour is encountered in which positions along that row or column. For example, a green 1 means the first colour encountered moving from the edge of the grid along the row or column is green, while a blue 2 means the second colour encountered is blue.

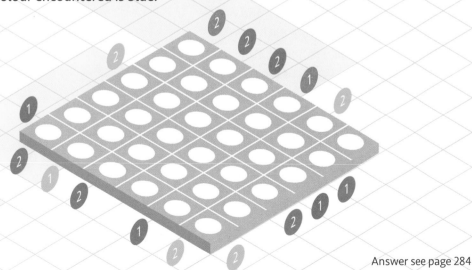

Answer see page 284

Test 10

01

Place a letter from A to H into every square, so that no letter repeats in any row or column. Identical letters cannot be in diagonally touching squares.

Answer see page 284

	A	G	C	H	E		
F							
H		D					F
B				H			
E							E
	H	A					A
					F		D
		B	F	E	A	B	C

Answer see page 284

02

Draw paths to join pairs of matching coloured shapes. Paths can only travel in straight lines between the centres of squares, and no more than one path can enter any square. Paths cannot touch or cross.

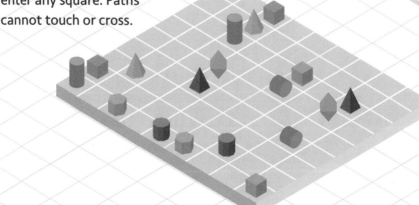

03 Write a number in each empty block so that every block is equal to the sum of the two blocks immediately below it.

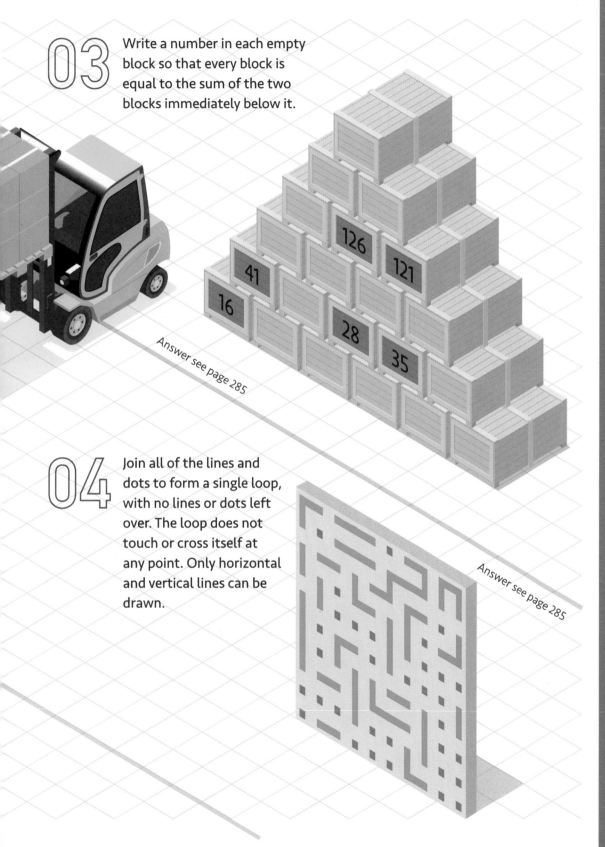

126

121

41

16

28

35

Answer see page 285

04 Join all of the lines and dots to form a single loop, with no lines or dots left over. The loop does not touch or cross itself at any point. Only horizontal and vertical lines can be drawn.

Answer see page 285

05 Place a number from 1 to 8 once each into every row and column of the grid, while obeying the region clues. The value at the top left of each bold-lined region must be obtained when all of the numbers in that region have the given operation (+, −, ×, ÷) applied between them. For − and ÷ operations, begin with the largest number in the region and then subtract or divide by the other numbers in the region in any order.

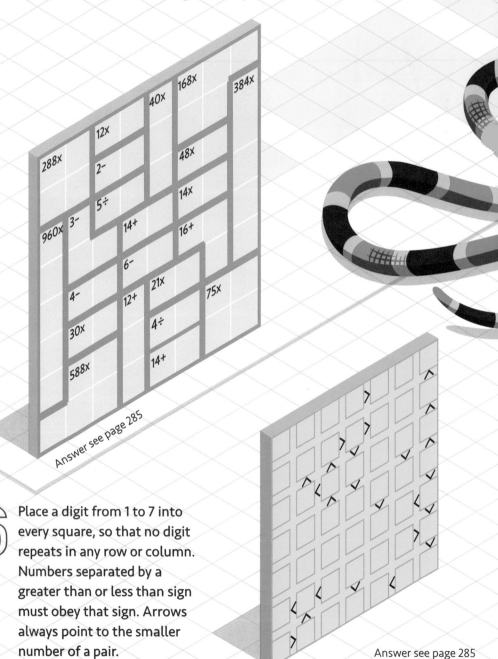

Answer see page 285

06 Place a digit from 1 to 7 into every square, so that no digit repeats in any row or column. Numbers separated by a greater than or less than sign must obey that sign. Arrows always point to the smaller number of a pair.

Answer see page 285

07 Place a colour into each empty square so that every colour appears once in each row, column and bold-lined jigsaw shape.

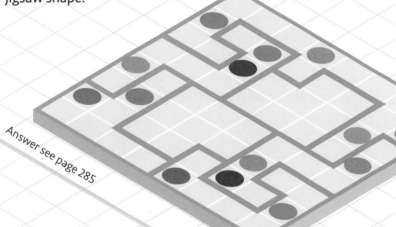

Answer see page 285

08

Shade some squares to form a snake that starts and ends at the snake eyes. Numbers outside the grid specify the number of squares in their row or column that contain part of the snake. A snake is a single path of adjacent shaded squares that does not branch. Shaded squares cannot touch, except for the immediately preceding and following squares in the snake. Shaded squares also cannot touch diagonally, except as necessary for the snake to turn a corner.

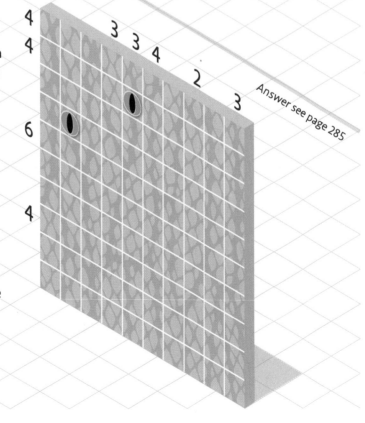

Answer see page 285

09 Place numbers from 1 to 9 so that each row, column and bold-lined 3x3 box contains one of each number. Numbers from 1 to 3 must be placed in regular grid squares; numbers from 4 to 6 must be placed in grid squares that contain a green circle; and numbers from 7 to 9 must be placed in grid squares that contain an orange circle.

Answer see page 285

10 Draw a single loop by joining some dots so that each numbered square has the specified number of adjacent line segments. Dots can only be joined by horizontal or vertical lines, and the loop cannot touch, cross or overlap itself in any way.

Answer see page 285

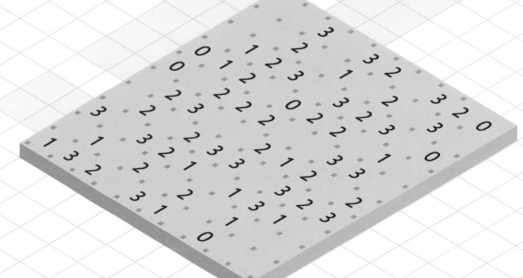

11 Join dots with horizontal and vertical lines to form a single path which does not touch or cross itself at any point. The start and end of the path are given by the red circles. Numbers outside the grid specify the number of dots in their row or column that are visited by the path.

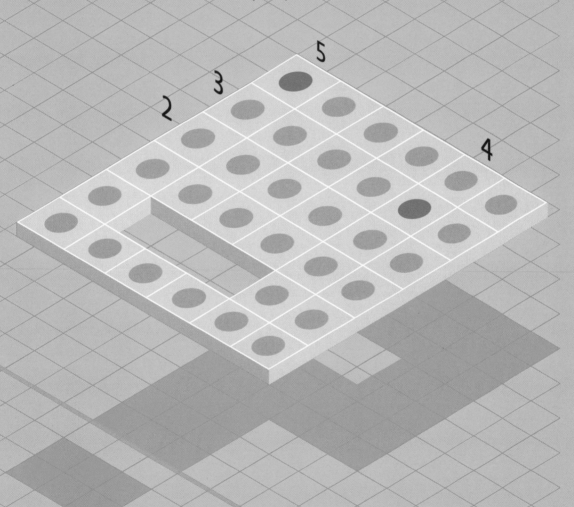

Answer see page 285

12 Place a digit from 1 to 5 into every square, so that no digit repeats in any row or column inside the grid. Place digits in such a way that each given clue number outside the grid represents the number of digits that are "visible" from that point, looking along that clue's row or column. A digit is visible if there is no higher digit preceding it.

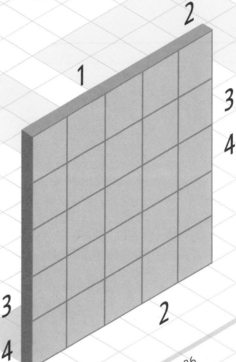

Answer see page 286

Answer see page 286

13 Place a number from 1 to 7 once each in every row and column. Values outside the grid give the total of the numbers in each of the indicated diagonals.

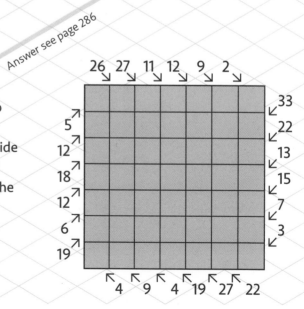

14 Draw along the dashed lines to divide the grid to form a complete set of standard dominoes, with exactly one of each domino. A "0" represents a blank on a traditional domino. Use the check-off chart (right) to help you keep track of which dominoes you've placed.

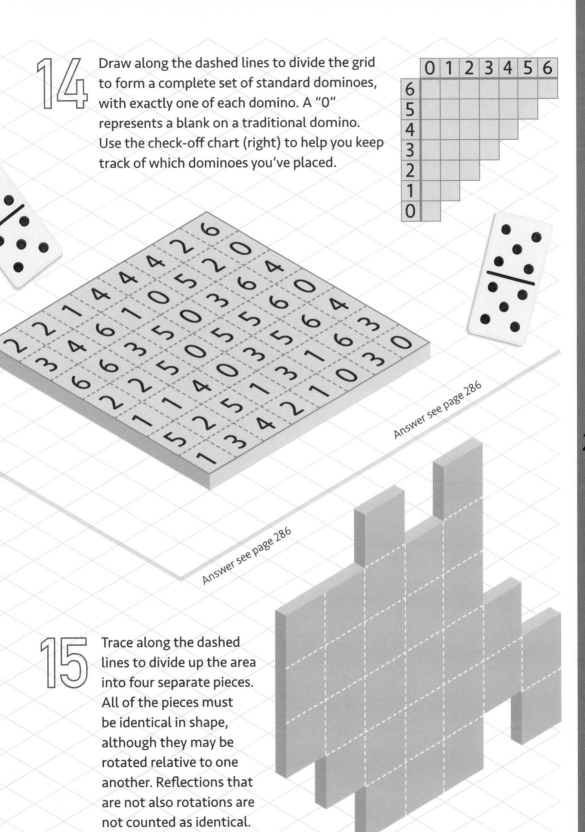

	0	1	2	3	4	5	6
6							
5							
4							
3							
2							
1							
0							

Answer see page 286

Answer see page 286

15 Trace along the dashed lines to divide up the area into four separate pieces. All of the pieces must be identical in shape, although they may be rotated relative to one another. Reflections that are not also rotations are not counted as identical.

16 Place a digit from 1 to 8 into every square, so that each digit appears once in every row and column. Squares separated by a pink peg must contain two consecutive numbers, such as 2 and 3. Squares separated by a red peg must contain numbers where one is twice the value of the other, such as 2 and 4. All possible dots are given, so if there is no dot, then a neighbouring pair can be neither consecutive nor have one be twice the value of the other. Where 1 and 2 are neighbours, either a red peg or a pink peg might be given, but not both.

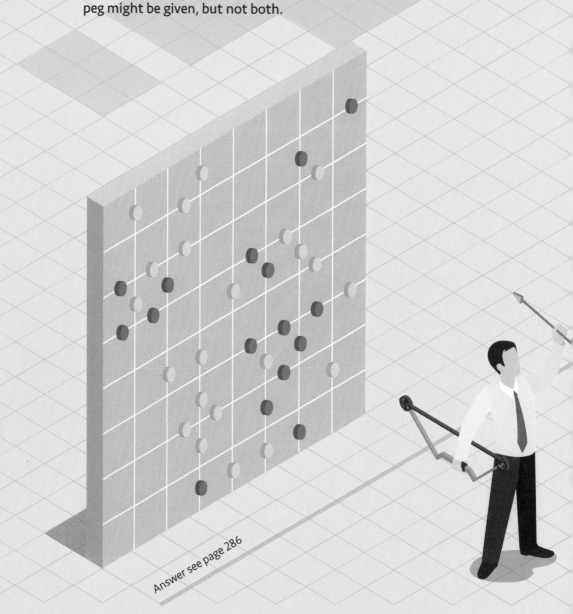

Answer see page 286

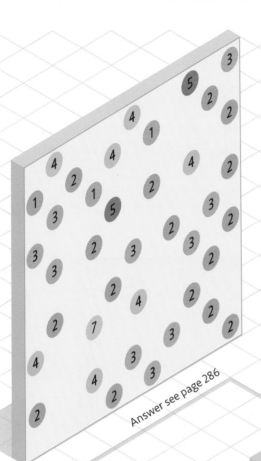

17

Draw horizontal and vertical lines along each row and column of circles to join circled numbers. Each circle contains a number which specifies the number of lines that connect to it. No more than two lines may join any pair of circles. Lines may not cross other lines or circles. All circles must be joined in such a way that you can travel from any circle to any other circle by following one or more lines.

Answer see page 286

Answer see page 286

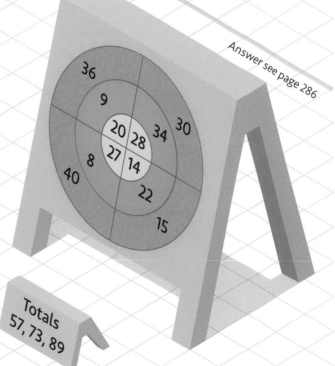

18

Can you make each of the totals shown? For each total, choose one number from the outer ring, one number from the middle ring, and one number from the inner ring. The three numbers must add up to the given total.

Totals
57, 73, 89

19 Place a digit from 1 to 9 into each yellow square, so that no digit repeats in any consecutive horizontal or vertical run of squares. Each horizontal or vertical run has a total given immediately to its left or above, respectively. The digits in that run must add up to the given total.

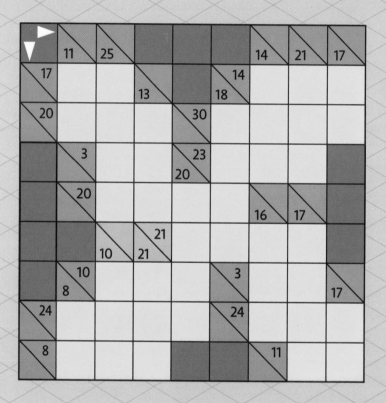

Answer see page 286

20

Reveal a hidden picture by shading some squares, while obeying the clues at the start of each row or column. The clues provide, in reading order, the length of every run of consecutive shaded squares in each row and column. There must be a gap of at least one empty square between each run of shaded squares in the same row or column.

					2	2		1		1					
			3		2	3	2	2	2	2	2				
		2	2	3	1	1	3	1	1	1	3	4	3	3	2
	3	1	1	3	1	1	1	1	4	1	1	4	1	1	1
3															
3, 2															
2, 2															
2, 1, 2															
2, 2, 3															
1, 2															
2, 2, 4															
1, 3, 1															
2, 3, 1															
2, 2, 2															
1, 1															
3, 3															
7															
1, 1															
4, 4, 2															

Answer see page 286

21 Write a number in each empty block so that every block is equal to the sum of the two blocks immediately below it.

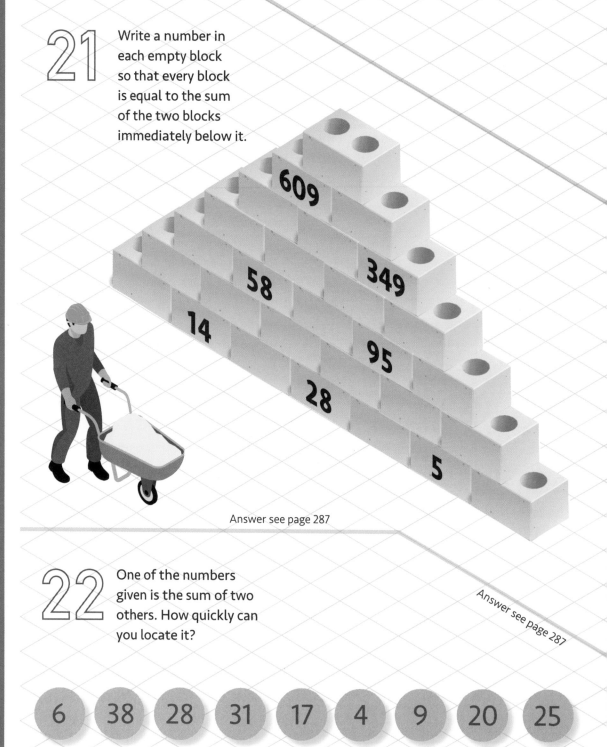

609

349

58

14

95

28

5

Answer see page 287

22 One of the numbers given is the sum of two others. How quickly can you locate it?

Answer see page 287

6   38   28   31   17   4   9   20   25

23

Fill the grid so that each row and column contains the colours red, blue, green and yellow, and two empty squares. The coloured digits surrounding the grid indicate which colour is encountered first along that row or column. For example, a red 1 means the first colour encountered moving from the edge of the grid along the row or column is red, while a blue 2 means the second colour encountered is blue.

Answer see page 287

24

(Stories of the Empire State Building ÷ syllables in a haiku) x (Number of years of the Ming dynasty – number of years of Tsar Nicholas II's reign)

Answer see page 287

25 Three of the four animals given are odd in relation to the other three. Which of the four is a perfect match with the other three?

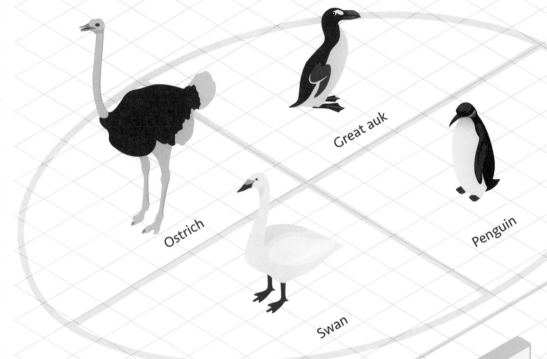

Great auk

Ostrich

Penguin

Swan

Answer see page 287

26 Fill the grid with the digits 1-9 to make the sums work. Solve from left to right and top to bottom in sequence – rules regarding the order of mathematical operations do not apply.

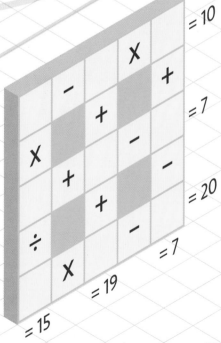

= 10

= 7

= 20

= 7

= 15

= 19

Answer see page 287

Fit the listed numbers
into the grid.

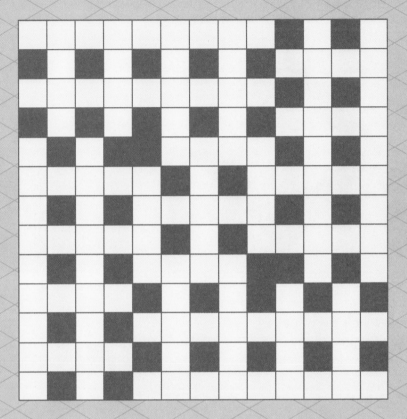

4 digits	5 digits	9 digits
1203	21964	143896092
1348	28056	231985053
1458	29176	235196740
1467	39841	332370538
3297	41139	355649082
3751	43870	538626044
4274	62931	584179371
4384	64115	701429346
4504	74309	
6598	78310	
8599		
8762		

Answer see page 287

28

Fill in the blank shape following the below rules:

All edges of the frame have moved location, and blue, in the top half of the frame, is between yellow and green.

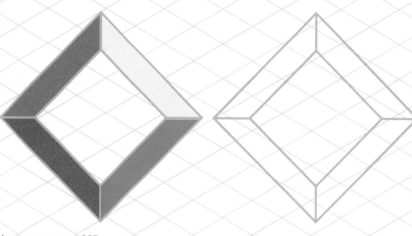

Answer see page 287

29

What is the value of pink?

Answer see page 287

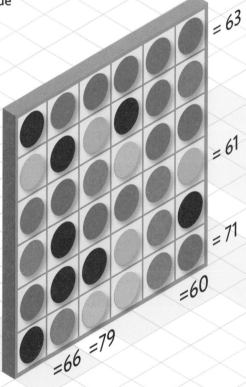

= 63

= 61

= 71

=60

=66 =79

30 The four images follow a pattern. Which option continues the sequence?

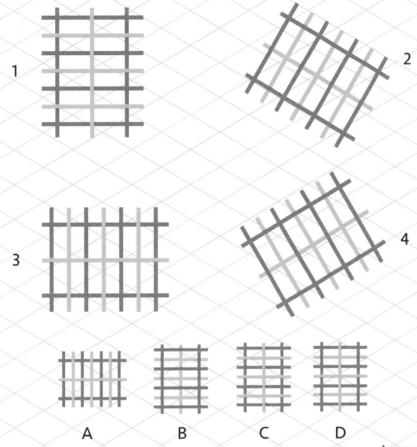

A   B   C   D

Answer see page 287

Answer see page 287

What number completes the sequence?

1   2   0   3   -1   4   -2   ?

32

In one of the busiest storm seasons in decades, the weather presenters were kept very busy. From the information given, work out each presenter's full name, the storm they revealed news about, and in which month and on which day of the week.

Jenny Snow broke news of her storm, which was neither Connor nor Eamonn, on an earlier day of the week than Paul. Paul announced his storm, which wasn't Bronagh, in March. News of Deirdre, January's storm, didn't break on Monday or Wednesday. The male presenter surnamed Rainbow presented on Friday; Tommy presented on Wednesday, but he wasn't the forecaster who announced September's storm. Thursday's presenter was Maria, but she wasn't surnamed Blizzard. Blizzard presented in November, but not about Bronagh. Storm Eamonn was first mentioned on a Friday, but not by Frost.

Answer see page 288

33

We've given you two separate equations. Each uses the same digits and each of the mathematical operations +, −, x and ÷. Use each of the given numbers to complete each equation. Solve in sequence from left to right – rules regarding the order of mathematical operations do not apply.

Answer see page 288

4 7 10 14 20

$$\bigcirc \div \bigcirc \times \bigcirc - \bigcirc + \bigcirc = 31$$

$$\bigcirc - \bigcirc \times \bigcirc \div \bigcirc + \bigcirc = 12$$

34 The manager of a chocolate factory has spotted a malfunction in the manufacturing process. Boxes of chocolates, each containing fifty chocolates, are packed in groups of eighteen. Yesterday, one out of each set of eighteen boxes contained one extra chocolate, so it is marginally heavier. It is impossible to tell by hand which is the heaviest box out of the eighteen. The manager offers a reward to anyone who can devise a process to locate the box containing the extra chocolate without opening the individual boxes. You receive the reward for suggesting a three-stage process using an industrial balance scale. What is the process?

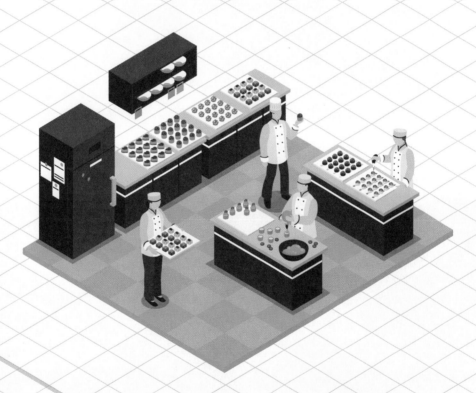

Answer see page 288

35 The first two scales
shown are balanced.
How many triangles
are needed to
balance the third?

1

2

3

Answer see page 288

36 Each set of numbers represents the name of a one-time-only Wimbledon Men's champion, the letters of which have been encoded according to the telephone number pad shown. What are the names?

5539866439488
46726482646476842
742427357254235
26373242774
642423578424
7282274
2784872743

Answer see page 288

37 Identify the mystery number. Compare the information beside the given numbers. Each digit that appears in the mystery number is marked by a dot. Green indicates a digit in the correct position, red if not. Here, 3825 shares two digits with the mystery number, but only one digit is in the correct position.

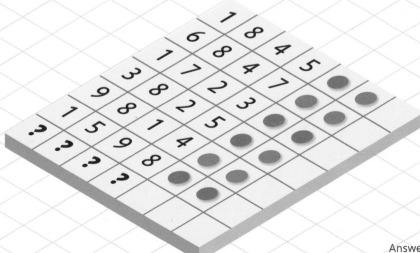

Answer see page 288

38

All the answers in this "crossword" are numbers. The unclued answer is a date (month, day, year) of significance in animation.

1	2		3		4		5		6	7
8							9	10		
			11	12		13				
14										
				15	16		17		18	
19		20	21				22			
23				24		25				
						26	27			
28	29		30		31					
32							33			34
35			36						37	

Across

1 4% of 9 Across
4 A quarter of 8 Across
6 Square root of 31 Down
8 9 Across + 1 Down
9 First half of 33 Across x 2 x 3 x 4 x 5
11 UNCLUED
14 569 x half a gross
15 645,298 + 23 Across
19 8 Across + 1 less than 34 Down
22 27 Down – 33 Across – 47
23 50,813 x 17 Down
26 15,109 x first digit of 5 Down
28 10,342,247 x 3
32 20% of 10 Down
33 246 + 397 + 1186 + 12 Down
35 $3^2 + 4^2 + 5^2$
36 151 x 4
37 Square root of 1369

Down

1 First two digits of 3 Down
2 18 Down x last digit of 25 Down
3 1 Across squared
4 Digits in even positions, in order, of 18 Down
5 Decreasing consecutive numbers
6 A palindrome
7 (13 Down x 957) + (12 x 47)
10 20 Down x 5 – (23 x 85)
12 Romans' CLXXXIII
13 25 Down – 100
16 Anagram of 29 Down
17 21 Down – 21 Down reversed
18 5,876,439 – 4,253,826
19 1267 x 185
20 101^2
21 3 x 34 Down
24 Consecutive ascending even numbers
25 4 Across + 5 Down
27 One-eighth of 14 Across
29 Degrees in a triangle
30 6 Down + seasons in a year
31 29 Down + 36 Across
34 37 Across – 20% of 35 Across

Answer see page 288

39 Which option most accurately completes the pattern?

is to **DANUBE** as  is to

Vienna

Budapest

TIBER	**VLATAVA**	**DANUBE**	**RHINE**	**AMSTEL**
A	B	C	D	E

Answer see page 288

Answer see page 288

40 Fill the 3x3 grid with each of the listed colours as directed: red, orange, yellow, green, blue, purple, pink, brown, black. All references refer to the same row or column, so that "A is above B" means A and B are in the same column, while "C is to the right/left of D" means C and D are in the same row. Yellow is above green, which is to the left of blue and pink. Pink is above orange, which is to the right of purple. Black is above blue and to the left of red. Green is above brown.

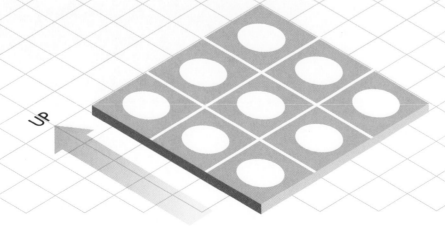

THE ANSWERS

Test 1

01

5	1	2	4	3
2	4	3	5	1
3	2	4	1	5
1	3	5	2	4
4	5	1	3	2

02

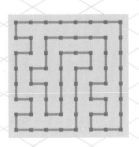

03

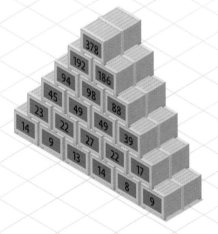

378
192 186
94 98
45 49 88
23 49
14 22 49 39
9 27
13 22
14 17
8
9

04

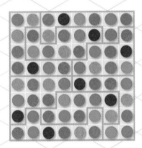

05

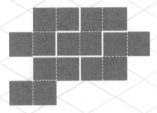

4÷ 1	4	2− 5	3− 6	3	4− 2
2− 2	1	3	15x 5	200x 4	6
4	22+ 2	6	3	1	5
6	3	3+ 1	2	5	4x 4
15x 3	5	2	4x 4	36x 6	1
5	24x 6	4	1	2	3

06

07

08

| | 3 | 2 | 3 | 4 | 3 | 3 | 1 | 5 | 4 | 5 |

09

	5	2	3	2	1	
5	1	2	3	4	5	1
2	2	5	4	1	3	3
3	3	4	2	5	1	2
2	4	1	5	3	2	3
1	5	3	1	2	4	2
	1	3	2	3	2	

10

25 11 5 10 3

	5	4	2	1	6	3	14
5	2	1	6	5	3	4	12
6	6	3	5	4	2	1	12
9	4	6	1	3	5	2	7
14	1	5	3	2	4	6	5
23	3	2	4	6	1	5	5

3 3 13 21 9

11

5	0	2	1	3	3	0
3	3	2	4	6	5	4
2	2	4	6	5	1	2
0	4	1	6	1	6	3
5	6	1	5	2	3	0
6	3	2	0	5	5	4
0	0	6	1	5	1	4

12

C	B	F	E	D	A
E	D	A	C	B	F
B	F	E	D	A	C
A	C	B	F	E	D
F	E	D	A	C	B
D	A	C	B	F	E

13

3	3	3		0
1			2	
1		3		2	1
3	2		3		1
	1				1
			1		1
	0		2	3	1

14

7	8	5	4	1	2	3	6	9
3	6	2	9	8	7	5	1	4
1	9	4	6	5	3	2	7	8
4	2	3	1	7	8	6	9	5
9	1	8	5	3	6	7	4	2
6	5	7	2	4	9	1	8	3
8	7	1	3	2	4	9	5	6
2	4	9	7	6	5	8	3	1
5	3	6	8	9	1	4	2	7

15

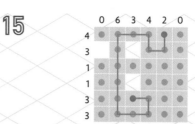

16

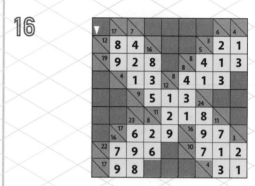

17

18

19

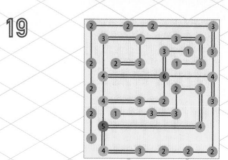

20

50 = 8 + 15 + 27
62 = 11 + 19 + 32
73 = 12 + 29 + 32

21

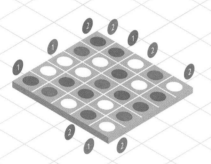

22   **21** (18 + 3)

23

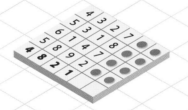

24

25   An elephant is vegetarian; a great white shark is a fish, not a mammal; a gorilla doesn't have a tail. The dolphin is a carnivorous, tailed mammal.

26

9	–	5	+	6	= 10
÷		÷		÷	
3	x	1	x	2	= 6
+		+		+	
8	–	4	x	7	= 28
= 11		= 9		= 10	

27   **221.** (The sequence is made up of the product of two neighbouring prime numbers, in an ascending order – 2 x 3, 3 x 5, 5 x 7, 7 x 11, 11 x 13, 13 x 17.)

28

3	6	5		6	4	3	4	4
4		4		9		1		7
3	4	9	7	2		1	2	3
	3		5			2		6
3	2	7	4		3	2	7	5
7		1		8		2		
1	9	4		6	9	4	5	8
6		9		8		9		2
5	3	2	8	5		5	6	7

29

30   **45.** (7, 12, 14).

31   Three. (Triangle = 1, cube = 2, cylinder = 3, hexagon = 4)

32
Captain Picky, 21 months, Urania, space walks.
Commander Cork, 19 months, Selena, filter cleaning.
Sergeant Starr, 16 months, Venus, experiments.

33
$9 \div 3 + 12 - 5 \times 6 = 60$
$12 - 6 \times 3 \div 9 + 5 = 7$

34
B. Double the number of sides in the second polygon as in the first.

35
A. The image rotates clockwise by 90° each time, with an extra yellow stripe introduced each time, and in the next position along. Red stripes alternate between being below and above.

36
Adele, Cher, Madonna, Rihanna, Shakira, Beyonce.

37

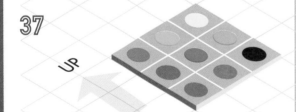

UP

38

3	2	5	3	8	1	
4	1		4		6	4
	1	6	1	9	0	7
1		6		4		6
3	9	1	1	5	8	
5	7		1		1	6
	7	1	6	5	3	9

1/6/1907: Maria Montessori opens her first school.

39
44: $(14 \times 5) - (8 + 18)$

40
Three times a year (every $3 \times 5 \times 7 = 105$ days); April 15th.

Test 2

01

02

03

390
204 186
105 99 87
53 52 47 40
28 25 27 20 20
15 13 12 15 5 15

04

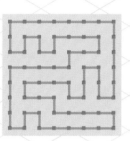

05

18+ 4	5	6	3	2x 2	1
3x 3	1	6+ 2	5– 6	160x 4	5
120x 5	5+ 3	4	1	18x 6	2
6	2	4+ 1	10x 5	3	4
1	4	3	2	11+ 5	6
4– 2	6	60x 5	4	1	3

06

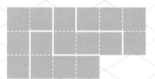

07

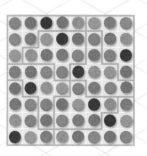

08

6 5 4 4 5 2 3 2 3 3

8
6
2
8
2
2
3
3
3
0

09

	3	2	2	4	1	
3	3	4	2	1	5	1
2	4	1	5	2	3	2
1	5	3	1	4	2	3
2	2	5	4	3	1	4
4	1	2	3	5	4	2
	3	2	3	1	2	

10

21 14 7 10 6

2	3	4	1	5	6	22
6	1	2	4	3	5	17
1	2	5	6	4	3	6
3	4	1	5	6	2	6
5	6	3	2	1	4	1
4	5	6	3	2	1	

2, 9, 6, 8, 23

4 10 15 11 13

11

1	6	3	1	4	0	4	3
2	5	0	5	6	6	4	1
3	5	1	2	1	6	2	3
3	1	1	5	5	3	2	1
2	2	4	2	6	6	0	3
4	4	6	5	0	4	4	5
0	3	2	5	6	0	0	0

12

B	D	C	F	A	E
F	A	E	B	D	C
E	B	D	C	F	A
C	F	A	E	B	D
A	E	B	D	C	F
D	C	F	A	E	B

13

1 1 0
2 1 1
3 2 2 3
2 3 2 2
1 2 3
3 2 3

14

8	4	1	5	7	2	9	3	6
9	2	3	6	8	1	7	4	5
7	5	6	9	4	3	8	2	1
2	3	5	7	9	6	4	1	8
1	6	8	3	2	4	5	9	7
4	9	7	8	1	5	3	6	2
6	7	2	4	5	9	1	8	3
5	1	4	2	3	8	6	9	7
3	8	9	1	6	7	2	5	4

15

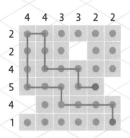

16

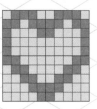

17

18

5	7	3	2	8	6	1	4
8	2	6	3	1	4	7	5
3	6	4	8	7	1	5	2
6	4	8	5	2	7	3	1
2	3	7	1	5	8	4	6
1	8	5	4	3	2	6	7
4	5	1	7	6	3	2	8
7	1	2	6	4	5	8	3

19

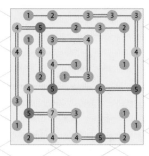

20

44 = 10 + 18 + 16
66 = 32 + 18 + 16
88 = 40 + 11 + 37

21

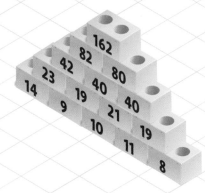

22

28 (12 + 16)

23

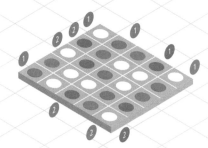

24

100: (1800 ÷ 9) − (88 + 12)

25 Tokyo isn't in Europe; Paris isn't on the coast; Venice isn't a capital city. Dublin is a European coastal capital.

26

3	+	5	–	1	= 7
x		x		x	
9	+	8	+	6	= 23
–		÷		+	
7	–	4	x	2	= 6
= 20		= 10		= 8	

27 **945.** (The sequence is made up of the product of the previous number multiplied by the next ascending odd number – 1 x 1, 1 x 3, 3 x 5, 15 x 7, 105 x 9.)

28

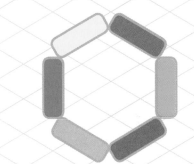

29

30 **47.** (8, 12, 15).

31 **D.** The number of dots in each stage increases by two; each image is symmetrical when folded along the diagonal from top right to bottom left.

32 $55^{55}/_5$

33 18 – 11 x 6 + 12 ÷ 9 = 6
18 ÷ 6 x 12 – 9 + 11 = 38

34 Addaya, pyramid, Horus, 8 years. Buneb, fortress, Amun, 4 years. Dedi, temple, Isis, 6 years.

35 Twelve. (Triangle = 1, hexagon = 4, cube plus cylinder = 4).

36 Phil Mickelson, Sergio Garcia, Jack Nicklaus, Tiger Woods, Arnold Palmer, Rory McIlroy

37

38

9	1		6	5	4		1	3
6	3	4		4		2	9	6
	2	4		9	2	2	5	
2		9	1	0		8	7	3
1	3	6	2		3	1	3	6
3	4	3		8	1	9		1
	5	1	2	9		3	9	
3	6	0		5		5	5	8
5	7		1	2	3		1	9

2/28/1935: Wallace Carruthers invents nylon.

39

E. Ignore the colours. Each constituent shape in the second image has two extra sides.

40

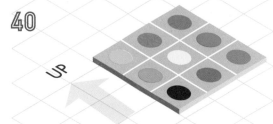

UP

Test 3

01

3 > 2	6	5 > 4	1
6	5	4	1	3 > 2
2 < 3	1	6 > 5	4
5	1	2	4	6	3
4	6	3	2	1	5
1	4 < 5	3 > 2	6

02

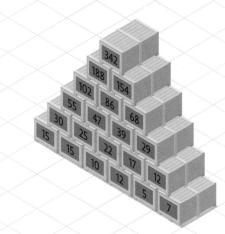

5	3	7	1	4	6	8	2	9
2	1	9	8	5	3	4	7	6
6	4	8	2	7	9	1	5	3
3	6	4	5	1	2	7	9	8
1	9	2	7	3	8	5	6	4
7	8	5	6	9	4	3	1	2
9	5	6	4	8	7	2	3	1
8	7	3	9	2	1	6	4	5
4	2	1	3	6	5	9	8	7

03

342

188 | 154

102 | 86

55 | 86 | 68

30 | 47 | 68

15 | 25 | 39 | 29

15 | 22 | 17 | 12

10 | 17 | 12

12 | 5

7

04

05

30x 2	5÷ 1	5	17+ 6	4	16+ 3	7
5	3	1	2	12+ 7	6	72x 4
13+ 7	6	4	1- 1	5	5+ 2	3
72x 4	245x 5	7	3	2	1	6
3	7	12x 6	5	252x 1	2+ 4	2
6	2÷ 4	2	7	3	11+ 5	1
1	2	3	4	13+ 6	7	5

06

Top: 16 17 10 4 6

Right side: 15, 23, 13, 2, 3

Left side: 3, 5, 17, 10, 17

3	4	5	1	2	6
1	6	3	5	4	2
6	1	4	2	3	5
5	2	1	3	6	4
4	3	2	6	5	1
2	5	6	4	1	3

Bottom: 2 9 14 14 10

07

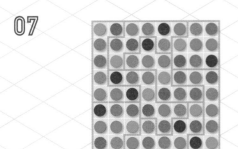

08

Top: 6 5   1 4 3   6

Left: 1, 6, 3, 2, 7

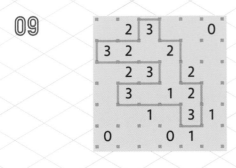

09

10

11

Top: 1 2

Left: 2, 3, 2

12

Top: 4

Left: 5, 1, 3

3	5	4	2	1
1	2	3	4	5
5	1	2	3	4
4	3	5	1	2
2	4	1	5	3

Right: 2

Bottom: 1 3

13

A	B	D	E	C	G	F
C	E	G	A	F	B	D
G	A	F	B	D	C	E
F	D	C	G	E	A	B
E	G	A	F	B	D	C
D	F	B	C	G	E	A
B	C	E	D	A	F	G

14

2	5	2	6	1	6	6	3
2	4	0	3	3	4	1	2
2	0	1	4	4	3	1	4
1	0	6	1	4	3	2	0
5	0	2	0	1	6	4	2
1	3	6	5	5	5	3	5
4	6	3	0	5	5	6	0

15

16

1	3	8	6	7	4	5	2
3	6	2	7	5	1	4	8
7	5	4	1	8	2	6	3
6	2	5	3	1	7	8	4
2	1	7	8	4	6	3	5
4	7	3	5	6	8	2	1
8	4	6	2	3	5	1	7
5	8	1	4	2	3	7	6

17

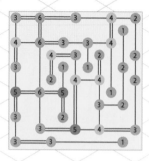

18

45 = 14 + 9 + 22
60 = 14 + 24 + 22
85 = 30 + 24 + 31

19

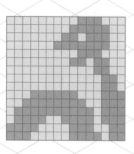

20

21

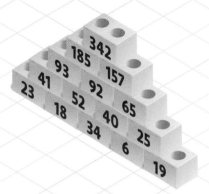

22   **26** (17 + 9)

23

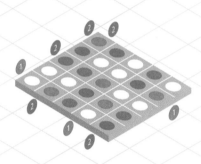

24   **13.** (The chance of the second Centurian not having the same birthday as the first is 99/100; the chance of the third not having the same birthday as either of the first two is 98/100, so the likelihood of these three Centurians not sharing a birthday is 0.99 x 0.98. Continue until the likelihood that Centurians don't share a birthday is less than 50%.)

25 The flute isn't a stringed instrument; the guitar isn't an orchestral instrument; the cello is a bass, rather than treble, instrument. The violin is a stringed orchestral instrument in the treble register.

26

1	x	8	x	4	= 32
+		÷		+	
9	–	2	+	7	= 14
÷		x		–	
5	x	6	÷	3	= 10
= 2		= 24		= 8	

27

	4	7	2	3		4	5	2	3	4
4		9		7	5	1		9		9
5	3	8	7	0		9	0	2	3	4
2			4		7	8				
6	5	2	3	3	7		6	4	2	7
8		9		4		7		6		7
6	7	5	3		3	5	0	3	8	6
		6		6		0				4
1	5	4	7	1		4	5	2	3	1
0		8		2	9	1		1		7
5	7	3	4	0		4	7	5	7	

28 **8.** (Each number in the sequence is the sum of the next two numbers in the sequence.)

29

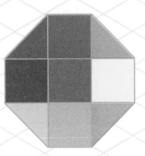

30 **30.** (5, 7, 8, 9).

31 Two. (Triangle = 5, cylinder = 3 cube = 2).

32 Yasmin, 45 years, Texas, carriage clock. Yehudi, 40 years, the Alps, fob watch. Yuri, 33 years, Rome, wristwatch.

33 28 – 7 ÷ 3 x 6 + 4 = 46
6 ÷ 3 + 28 – 7 x 4 = 92

34 **A.** Blue items rotate counter-clockwise by 45°, pink items by 90° and orange by 180°.

35 **A.** Primary colours move outwards by two spaces, orange and green alternate, and points follow the sequence of prime numbers.

36 Trump, Obama, Reagan, Carter, Hoover, Coolidge.

37

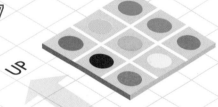

UP

38

	4	1	1	9	1	2		4
3	1		1	5		7	9	3
4		2	3		1	2	8	3
5	6	7	8	9	0		4	
	1	6	7		4	5	6	
	3		9	9	1	2	4	5
1	0	9	0		8	8		2
7	5	6		6	9		6	1
6		1	4	7	5	4	5	

10/4/1895: the first US Open golf tournament was held at Newport Golf Club, Rhode Island.

39   **111:** (97 − 42) + (7 × 8)

40

Test 4

01

1	<	2	6		3	<	5	>	4
		∧							
4	>	3	5	6		2		1
∧								
5		1	3	<	4	6		2
∧								
6		4	2	>	1	<	3	5
2		6	4	5		1		3
			∨	∨		∨		
3		5	1	2		4		6

02

7	4	8	3	9	2	6	5	1
1	9	6	8	5	4	2	3	7
2	5	3	1	7	6	8	4	9
4	1	2	7	3	8	5	9	6
5	6	9	2	4	1	3	7	8
3	8	7	9	6	5	4	1	2
9	3	5	6	8	7	1	2	4
6	2	4	5	1	9	7	8	3
8	7	1	4	2	3	9	6	5

03

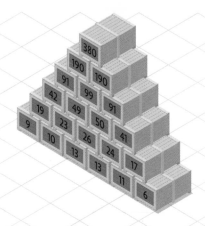

04

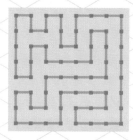

05

10+ 6	3− 7	1	3	84x 2	20x 4	105x 5
4	6x 2	6÷ 6	1	7	5	3
6x 2	3	1− 5	4	1	6	7
3	96x 4	210x 7	5	6	1	4− 2
1− 5	1	3	2− 2	4	4− 7	6
1	30x 6	2	12+ 7	5	3	5+ 4
7	5	4	1÷ 6	3	2	1

06

	17↓	17↓	15↓	4↓	2↓		
4→	4	1	6	5	3	2	11↙
3→	2	6	3	4	5	1	11↙
15→	3	2	4	6	1	5	15↙
11→	1	3	5	2	4	6	5↙
19→	5	4	2	1	6	3	4↙
	6	5	1	3	2	4	
	6↖	10↖	6↖	11↖	12↖		

07

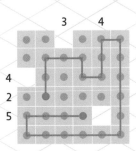

08

   4   5 7

4
1
4
3
6
4
3

09

3	3	3	3	2	2	3	3
1		1		0			1
3	2		3	1			2
2				0		1	3
3	3		3		3		2
2		2	1		3		2
3			2		2		1
3	3	2	3	3	2	3	3

10

11

    3   4

4
2
5

12

2
1	5	4	3	2	4
5	4	2	1	3	

4
2	1	3	4	5	
4	3	5	2	1	3

2
3	2	1	5	4
3

13

F	E	C	G	D	A	B
G	A	D	B	E	C	F
E	B	G	C	F	D	A
D	C	F	A	B	G	E
A	G	B	E	C	F	D
B	D	A	F	G	E	C
C	F	E	D	A	B	G

14

2	0	1	0	0	0	0	5
2	4	1	5	5	6	2	3
4	1	3	6	5	6	0	3
4	2	1	5	0	3	2	3
4	4	5	6	4	3	6	0
3	4	5	2	4	6	2	1
1	6	5	6	2	3	1	1

15

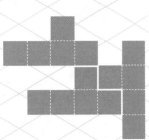

16

6	8	1	7	2	4	3	5
5	3	8	2	7	1	6	4
1	4	6	3	8	5	2	7
7	6	5	4	3	8	1	2
2	1	4	6	5	7	8	3
8	7	3	5	6	2	4	1
3	5	2	1	4	6	7	8
4	2	7	8	1	3	5	6

17

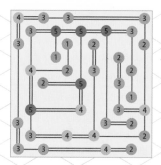

21

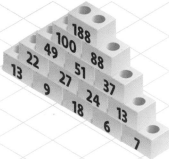

18

60 = 20 + 22 + 18
88 = 20 + 33 + 35
100 = 40 + 22 + 38

22

18 (4 + 14)

19

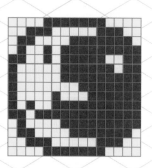

23

24

13. (8, 9, 11).

25

Venus is a goddess, not a god; Cupid is not a planet; Uranus is Greek not Roman. Jupiter is a planet named after a male Roman god.

20

26

3	x	9	–	7	= 20
x		+		x	
4	x	6	÷	8	= 3
x		–		–	
2	x	1	x	5	= 10
= 24		= 14		= 51	

27

5. (The sequence depends on the difference between increasing prime numbers; add the prime number to the numbers in odd positions in the sequence, subtract from those in even positions. The solution is therefore 18 − 13.)

28

1	5	5		1	2	3	7	9	4
2		7		4		9		2	2
3	6	5	7	5		6	3	0	4	2
4		1		8		6			3
9	6	2	8		3	2	1	5	8	4
8		3		2		0		7		0
7	0	6	8	9	4		3	4	5	8
6				6		1		3		7
9	4	1	7	5		6	3	2	5	6
0		2		8		5		1		9
	6	0	3	7	8	4		5	9	9

29

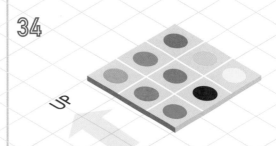

30

48: (500 ÷ 125) x (5 + 7)

31

B. Red and blue move clockwise one space, yellow and green counter-clockwise by one space. Where they coincide, the colour they produce when mixed is shown.

32

5	2		4	5	7		1	6
6	2	5	8		2	2	9	7
	3	2	6	1	9	2	3	
1	5	9		8		7	6	6
1		1	4	2	4	1		3
3	1	8		8		5	4	0
	3	4	2	0	3	2	1	
2	2	7	7		5	6	1	7
3	8		9	8	7		3	2

3/26/1923: Sarah Bernhardt died.

33

Veronica, laptop, $299, Herbert Wilson. Maurice, camera, $199, Favourites. Lucinda, dress, $129, Lewis John.

34

UP

35

8; 1.

36

15 − 7 x 4 + 8 ÷ 5 = 8
8 ÷ 4 x 15 + 5 − 7 = 28

37

D. The first element is the binary equivalent of the second, decimal, element.

38

One cube. (Cube = 2, cylinder = 3, triangle = 6).

39

Benicio Del Toro, Roberto Benigni, Jean DuJardin, Christoph Waltz, Javier Bardem.

40

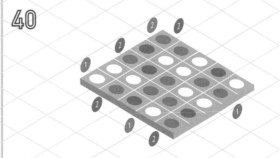

Test 5

01

3	2 >	1 <	6	4	5
1 <	3	6	5	2 <	4
4	1 <	5	2	6 >	3
6	5 >	4	1	3	2
5	4	2	3 >	1	6
2	6	3	4 <	5 <	1

02

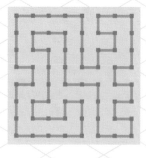

03

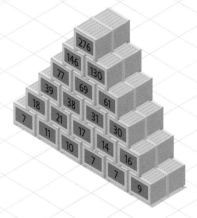

04

05

8x 2	7x 1	7	35x 5	120x 4	18x 6	3
4	3− 5	72x 3	7	6	10+ 2	6− 1
2÷ 6	2	4	11+ 3	5	1	7
3	13+ 4	6	2	21x 1	7	9+ 5
8+ 3	3	2− 2	6	7	9+ 5	4
7	6	5	5+ 1	3	4	3÷ 2
2− 5	7	1	4	5+ 2	3	6

06

10 21 15 3 3

4	2	6	5	1	3	19
3	4	1	6	5	2	16
6	1	4	2	3	5	13
1	5	2	3	4	6	3
2	3	5	4	6	1	4
5	6	3	1	2	4	

4, 5, 16, 8, 18 (left)

5 8 7 17 12

07

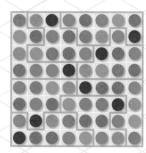

08

| | 2 | 5 | 4 | | 2 | | 5 | 5 |

09

4 2

4	1	5	3	2
5	2	3	1	4
2	3	4	5	1
1	5	2	4	3
3	4	1	2	5

2 1

10

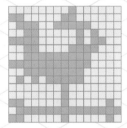

11

1	5	1	2	5	2	6	0
1	3	3	1	4	2	2	5
3	5	0	6	1	5	4	6
6	0	6	0	2	5	4	1
3	4	6	2	0	4	1	4
5	3	3	6	3	4	3	6
5	1	0	2	2	4	0	0

12

F	C	E	A	B	D	G
A	D	B	G	F	E	C
B	E	A	C	D	G	F
D	G	F	E	A	C	B
E	B	C	D	G	F	A
C	A	G	F	E	B	D
G	F	D	B	C	A	E

13

3	2	2	3			3	2	3
3	2		2		2	3	2	
2		1	1	3		2		2
3	3			1				
		3				3	3	
2	2		2	3	2			2
2	1	1		1		2	3	
3	3	3		3	2	1	3	

14

7	1	8	6	5	2	3	4	9
2	5	3	1	9	4	6	7	8
6	9	4	3	7	8	5	2	1
5	6	1	4	2	3	8	9	7
3	7	2	5	8	9	4	1	6
8	4	9	7	1	6	2	3	5
4	3	7	9	6	5	1	8	2
1	2	6	8	3	7	9	5	4
9	8	5	2	4	1	7	6	3

15

16

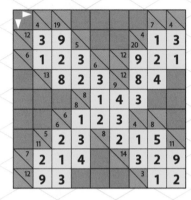

17

18

2	1	3	4	5	8	6	7
4	6	2	8	7	5	3	1
5	8	7	1	3	6	2	4
1	2	5	3	6	7	4	8
8	5	4	6	2	1	7	3
6	3	8	7	4	2	1	5
3	7	6	5	1	4	8	2
7	4	1	2	8	3	5	6

19

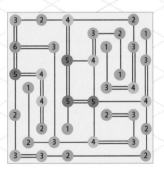

20

60 = 30 + 11 + 19
85 = 40 + 31 + 14
93 = 30 + 38 + 25

21

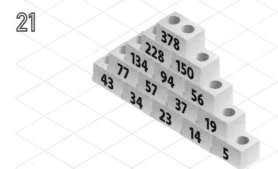

378
228 150
134 94
77 57 56
43 34 37 19
23 14
5

22 **28** (12 + 16)

23

24 **10:** (12 + 4) – (90 ÷ 15)

25 Oscar isn't a Shakespeare character; Oliver doesn't feature in the NATO phonetic alphabet; Juliet isn't a male name. Romeo is the name of a male Shakespeare character, and appears in the NATO phonetic alphabet.

26

8	x	4	÷	2	= 16
+		+		x	
9	x	7	÷	3	= 21
−		−		x	
5	+	1	÷	6	= 1

= 12   = 10   = 36

27 **129.** (Each number in the sequence increases by multiples of 6: 3 + 6 = 9, 9 + 12 = 21, 21 + 18 = 39, etc.)

28

6	5	6	9	8		6	3	4	8	8
7		2		4		9		3		3
2	0	8		5	3	4	0	7	2	4
5		3		0		5				9
	2	5	8	3	2		3	7	4	5
8		4		2	7	8		1		9
3	7	1	0		6	3	1	8	9	
4				6		4		3		3
9	2	4	3	7	0	0		5	9	1
5		2		5		5		2		4
6	5	6	3	2		2	3	1	8	9

29

30 3. (4, 5, 5).

31 **A.** One new element appears in sequence, with colours advancing accordingly (each new element in red).

32 **12** (3 presents per leg)

33 12 ÷ 3 + 24 − 4 x 2 = 48
24 ÷ 4 + 12 x 2 − 3 = 33

34 Cora, purple, bob, 15
questions, $10,000.
Dora, green, crop, 12
questions, $5,000.
Nora, yellow, ponytail,
7 questions, $8,000.

35 Two cubes. (Cube = 1, triangle
= 2, cylinder = 3, hexagon = 5)

36 Margaret Court, Virginia Wade,
Conchita Martinez, Martina
Hingis, Jana Novotna, Maria
Sharapova, Amelie Mauresmo,
Marion Bartoli.

37

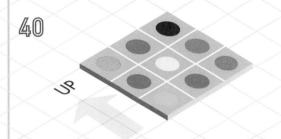

38

	1	5	8		4	7	1	
4	7		2	7	2		9	7
4	1	5	3	2	0	9		7
4	9	3		9	9	4	3	8
	3	6	1		2	3	4	
3	4	9	4	1		5	5	1
8		4	4	9	8	6	4	1
9	8		4	9	2		3	4
	2	1	1		3	5	2	

1/7/1934: Flash Gordon appears
in a comic strip for the first
time.

39 **B.** The upper shape becomes
the lower shape, and the one on
the right moves 90° clockwise
around the one on the left.

40

Test 6

01

4 >	3 >	2 >	1	5 <	6
5	1	6	3	4 >	2
6	2 >	1	4	3	5
1	5	3	2 <	6	4
3	6	4 <	5	2	1
2	4	5 <	6	1	3

02

03

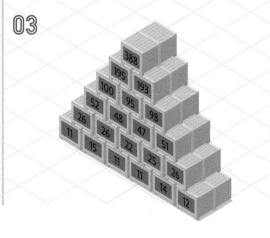

04

05

36x 2	28x 4	0- 3	150x 5	6	3÷ 1	7
3	7	4	1	5	8+ 6	2
6	1- 3	22+ 7	2	20x 4	5	3÷ 1
20x 5	2	6	4	21x 1	7	3
4	6÷ 6	1	7	2	3	15+ 5
6+ 1	5	60x 2	63x 3	7	2÷ 4	6
7÷ 7	1	5	6	3	2	4

06

B	C	D	A	G	F	E
E	F	G	B	D	C	A
D	A	C	F	E	G	B
C	G	E	D	B	A	F
F	B	A	G	C	E	D
G	D	F	E	A	B	C
A	E	B	C	F	D	G

07

08

7　3

3
3
3
4
4

4

09

4	1	2	5	3	
5	2	4	3	1	4
3	4	5	1	2	
2	3	1	4	5	
1	5	3	2	4	

3 (row3 left), 4 (row4 left)
Bottom: 4　　2　3

10

Top arrows: 19　15　19　21　7　3

	2	6	4	1	7	5	3	23
2	5	4	1	3	6	7	2	21
11	4	2	3	5	1	6	7	18
12	7	1	5	4	3	2	6	14
11	1	6	2	4	3	5		2
15	3	5	7	6	2	4	1	4
31	6	3	2	7	5	1	4	

Bottom arrows: 6　6　8　28　22　17

11

3	6	6	3	3	4	6	5
4	1	3	2	2	1	2	6
1	1	0	6	5	5	4	2
5	4	3	3	0	4	4	0
6	0	1	2	5	4	5	0
2	1	5	0	4	3	3	0
2	5	6	6	2	0	1	1

12

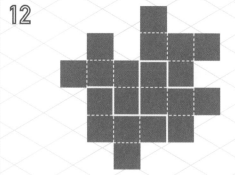

13

```
3 2     3 2 1 3
3   2     2 3
3 0 1 2 3 2   3
3   3   1   1 3
3 1     2   3 2
2   3 2 3 1 3 2
2 2       1   1
3 2 1 0     2 3
```

14

```
8 9 2 3 7 6 4 1 5
1 6 3 4 5 9 2 8 7
4 7 5 8 2 1 9 3 6
3 1 9 5 6 8 7 2 4
6 2 7 9 1 4 8 5 3
5 4 8 2 3 7 6 9 1
2 8 6 1 4 5 3 7 9
7 3 1 6 9 2 5 4 8
9 5 4 7 8 3 1 6 2
```

15

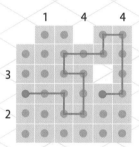

16

```
2 8 7 4 1 6 3 5
8 4 1 7 3 2 5 6
1 3 5 2 8 4 6 7
7 6 4 3 5 8 2 1
4 5 3 6 2 7 1 8
3 7 8 5 6 1 4 2
6 1 2 8 4 5 7 3
5 2 6 1 7 3 8 4
```

17

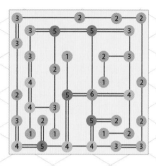

18

44 = 15 + 9 + 20
67 = 15 + 27 + 25
77 = 11 + 27 + 39

19

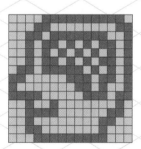

20

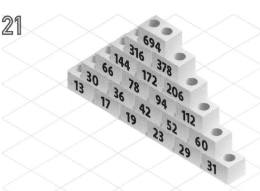

21

22

23 (9 + 14)

23

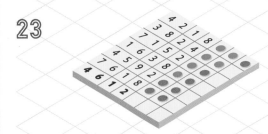

24

3, 7, 9, 12.

25

Nine triangles. (Triangle = 2, cube = 7, cylinder = 8)

26

Sting, Prince, Bono, Eminem, Drake, Seal, Meat Loaf.

27

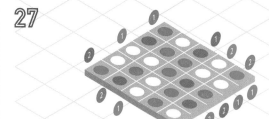

28

Squash is not an Olympic sport; handball is exclusively a team sport, and involves no racquet, bat or club; golf is an exclusively outdoor sport. Tennis is an Olympic sport with a racquet which can be played indoors.

29

6	x	5	÷	2	= 15
÷		+		x	
3	+	9	+	4	= 16
x		−		x	
8	+	7	−	1	= 14
= 16		= 7		= 8	

30

1113122113. Each successive number describes the previous number in the sequence: 13 describes the previous number, 3, as having one 3 (13), 1113 describes 13 as having one 1 and one 3 (1113), 3113 describes 1113 as having three 1s and one 3 (3113), etc.

31

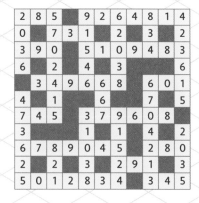

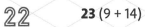

32

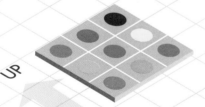

33   **68:** (64 ÷ 16) x (5 + 12)

34   **D.**

35

7	6	5	4		1	9	9	1
8	4		1	7	6		2	3
1	6	6	8		4	7	7	9
9	7			7	5	6		7
	9	1	5	1	8	9	8	
4		4	6	8			2	9
1	9	5	8		2	8	1	3
6	6		3	0	0		5	2
4	2	1	0		2	6	9	2

9/15/1898: the National Afro-
American Council founded, the
first national civil rights group.

36   Annie, pirate, Cheetahs, 3.55.
Bakeel, teddy bear, Falcons, 3.30.
Carly, bank manager, Jaguars,
3.42. Dan, fairy, Arrows, 4.17.

37

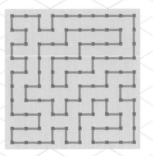

UP

38   **12**

39   9 – 4 x 8 + 36 ÷ 38 = 2
36 ÷ 4 x 8 – 38 + 9 = 43

40   **D.** Shapes are repeated in the
second element according the
the number of their sides.

01

1	4	7	6	5	2	3
3	7	6	1	2	5	4
6	3	5	7	1	4	2
4	5	2	3	6	1	7
5	6	4	2	7	3	1
2	1	3	5	4	7	6
7	2	1	4	3	6	5

02

3	2	6	1	8	5	4	9	7
4	5	9	2	7	3	6	8	1
7	1	8	6	9	4	2	5	3
9	7	4	3	2	1	8	6	5
6	8	1	9	5	7	3	4	2
5	3	2	4	6	8	1	7	9
1	6	5	7	4	2	9	3	8
2	9	7	8	3	6	5	1	4
8	4	3	5	1	9	7	2	6

03

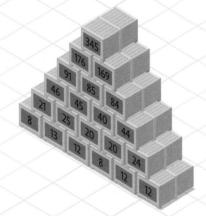

04

05

18+ 2	84x 1	90x 7	5	210x 4	6	3
4	5	3	7	224x 6	2	1
6	2	4	3	5	2− 1	7
140x 3	14x 4	6	1	7	70x 5	
1	3	16+ 2	6	7	5	4
7	6	5	840x 1	3	4	2
48x 5	7	1	4	2	3	6

06

Top: 25 11 18 12 9 6
Left: 7 6 7 23 18 17
Right: 42 13 21 15 5 1
Bottom: 4 8 8 23 17 31

7	1	3	5	4	2	6
5	2	6	1	3	4	7
2	6	5	3	1	7	4
6	5	4	2	7	1	3
3	4	1	7	2	6	5
1	3	7	4	6	5	2
4	7	2	6	5	3	1

07

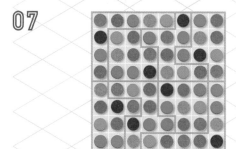

08

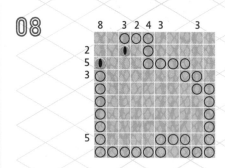

09

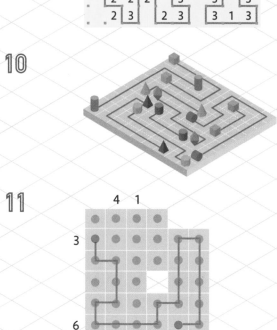

10

11

Top: 4 1
Left: 3 … 6

12

Top: 4 1
Bottom: 4 2

5	1	4	2	3	3
4	3	2	1	5	
2	4	5	3	1	3
3	5	1	4	2	3
1	2	3	5	4	4

Left clues: 3 (row3), 4 (row5)

13

D	G	F	C	H	E	B	A
A	H	E	B	F	C	D	G
F	B	A	D	E	G	H	C
C	D	G	H	B	A	E	F
H	E	C	A	D	F	G	B
B	F	D	G	C	H	A	E
G	C	B	E	A	D	F	H
E	A	H	F	G	B	C	D

14

3	4	0	4	0	6	5	5
6	1	5	4	5	0	1	3
3	3	1	2	3	2	4	2
1	3	6	6	6	1	5	4
3	2	6	0	2	0	0	6
3	0	5	6	2	2	4	0
4	1	5	2	5	4	1	1

15

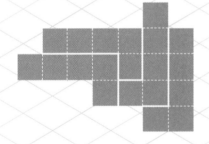

16

8	6	7	5	4	1	2	3
6	3	4	8	1	2	5	7
3	7	2	4	6	5	1	8
7	1	5	3	2	4	8	6
2	5	1	6	3	8	7	4
4	2	8	1	7	6	3	5
5	4	3	2	8	7	6	1
1	8	6	7	5	3	4	2

17

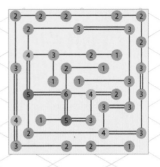

18

55 = 32 + 8 + 15
65 = 26 + 24 + 15
76 = 26 + 16 + 34

19

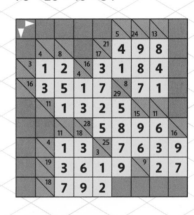

20

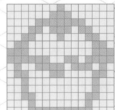

21

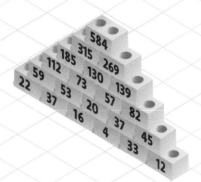

22   **37** (14 + 23)

23

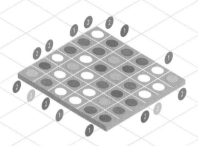

24   **2:** (4 x 5) ÷ (4 + 6)

25   The car is not not human-powered; the canoe is not land-based; the baby buggy passenger is not steering. The bicycle is a human-powered, land-based mode of transport with the passenger steering.

26

5	+	8	x	3	= 39
+		+		x	
1	+	9	-	6	= 4
+		x		-	
7	x	2	x	4	= 56
= 13		= 34		= 14	

27

2	9	4	8	1	3	5	0		8	4	9	2
7		9		0		7		3		5		2
1	2	9		2	8	9	6	2	0	3	1	3
6		5		3				4		0		7
	6	5	1	9		4	2	1	3	9	8	
5				3		9		2		1		3
5	0	3	0		7	3	8		6	4	3	2
5		4		3		5		7				5
	4	2	1	3	5	2		6	0	3	0	
5		2		4				2		2		6
2	7	9	4	1	9	3	0	4		3	4	8
3		1		5		6		5		8		3
9	9	7	9		4	9	2	8	1	5	3	0

28

29   4, 6, 11, 17.

30   **B.** Primary colours rotate clockwise in increasing increments of 60°, secondary colours rotate counter-clockwise to the next available.

31   **1165.** (The sequence alternates between addition and multiplication, with the relevant digit increasing by one each time: + 1, x 2, + 3, x 4, + 5 etc.)

32   Anna MacDonald, Thai, yellow. Dan Schmitt, Italian, blue. Fred Russo, Vegan, black. Nita Patel, French, red.

33   24 − 6 ÷ 3 x 12 + 8 = 80
12 ÷ 3 x 8 + 24 − 6 = 50

34   "I will be exiled to Elfrica."

35   Ten triangles. (Triangle = 2, cube = 3, cylinder = 8, hexagon = 10)

36   Penelope Cruz, Sophia Loren, Juliette Binoche, Ingrid Bergman, Marion Cotillard.

37

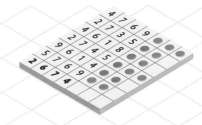

38

8	3	3		1	2	7	7	
4	1	9	5	9		3	4	3
3		1	1	8	5	1		2
6	1		7	3	0	4	4	4
	2	3	4		5	8	5	
6	4	1	8	9	6		1	7
6		1	2	5	3	3		1
1	4	8		1	1	6	6	3
	9	9	7	7		6	0	7

6/4/1896: Henry Ford test drives the Quadricyle, his first car.

39

E. The star is larger in the second image and rotated counter-clockwise by 90°.

40

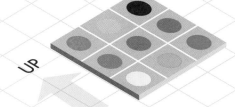

01

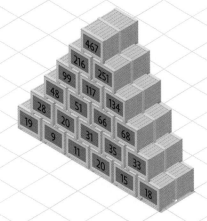

02

03

04

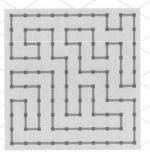

05

```
        3       3
    4  2  5  3  1   3
    3  1  2  4  5
 1  5  4  3  1  2   4
    1  5  4  2  3
 3  2  3  1  5  4   3
        2   3   2
```

06

D	A	B	H	F	C	E	G
C	G	D	A	E	H	B	F
A	F	H	C	B	G	D	E
H	E	A	G	D	F	C	B
G	C	F	B	H	E	A	D
F	B	G	E	A	D	H	C
E	H	C	D	G	B	F	A
B	D	E	F	C	A	G	H

07

1	5	0	1	0	0	5	4
3	4	3	6	6	2	0	5
5	4	1	3	6	5	5	2
1	5	5	0	1	2	4	2
0	6	1	4	4	6	6	4
3	3	3	1	4	3	2	3
2	2	6	1	0	2	0	6

08

09

7+ 2	5	60x 4	15x 3	7x 7	1176x 6	2x 1
18x 6	3- 4	3	5	1	7	2
3	1	5	192x 6	2	4	7
14+ 4	3	7	2	12+ 6	1	5
84x 1	7	2	4	60x 5	1- 4	2+ 6
35x 5	6	6x 1	7x 7	4	2	3
7	2	6	1	3	9+ 5	4

10

```
      22 20 12  7 12  7
    3  5  4  1  2  6  7   28
    5  7  2  3  1  4  6   26
3   7  2  3  6  4  5  1   15
10  2  6  1  4  3  7  5   11
18  1  4  7  5  6  3  2    4
7   4  1  6  7  5  2  3    4
15  6  3  5  2  7  1  4
22
       6  7  7 14 34 19
```

11

12

13

14

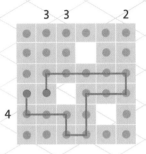

15

3 3 2

4

16

3	4	1	2	6	7	8	5
8	7	2	6	1	4	5	3
4	2	5	1	8	3	6	7
7	3	8	5	4	1	2	6
5	6	4	3	7	8	1	2
2	5	7	8	3	6	4	1
6	1	3	4	2	5	7	8
1	8	6	7	5	2	3	4

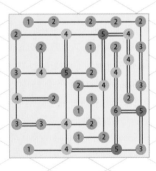

17

18

60 = 13 + 27 + 20
65 = 25 + 22 + 18
80 = 38 + 22 + 20

19

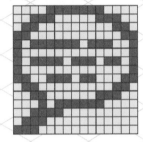

20

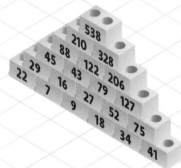

21

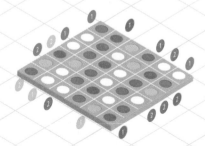

22 **32** (19 + 13)

23

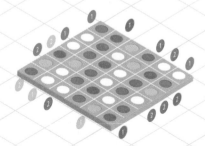

24 **48:** (3 × 8) + (4 + 20)

25 Eight hexagons. (Cylinder = 1, hexagon = 2, triangle = 3, cube = 4)

26 Romeo, Hamlet, Macbeth, Orlando, Falstaff, Orsino, Malvolio.

27

28 Canada is in the northern hemisphere; Mozambique is Portuguese-speaking, not English-speaking; New Zealand is an island nation. Namibia is an English-speaking, continental, southern hemisphere country.

29

1	+	7	x	8	= 64
x		x		x	
9	÷	3	x	6	= 18
x		−		÷	
2	+	5	−	4	= 3
= 18		= 16		= 12	

30

31

32 5. (9, 13, 17, 20.)

33 **A.**

34 **141.** (Each number in the sequence increases by successive square numbers: 1, 4, 9, 16 etc.)

35 **12.** (If 12 osprey caught 24 fish in 36 minutes, those same 12 osprey will catch 240 fish in 360 minutes. 360 minutes is double 180 minutes, so the 12 osprey will catch 120 fish in 180 minutes.)

36 100 − 25 ÷ 5 + 3 x 4 = 72
5 − 3 x 100 ÷ 4 + 25 = 75

37 *Dances with Cubs*, Twiggy Alan, Starr Bell, Wire Twerp. *Dry River*, Cameron James, Annie Okay, Wild Bill Hiccup. *Forgotten*, Martin Scores, Calamity June, Billy Goat. *Low Noon*, Alfred Hitchnot, Wild Rose, Big Britches.

38

8/6/1991: The first website went live.

39 **D.** The middle figure stays in the same position, the deepest figure becomes the nearest and vice versa, and left moves to right while right moves to left.

40

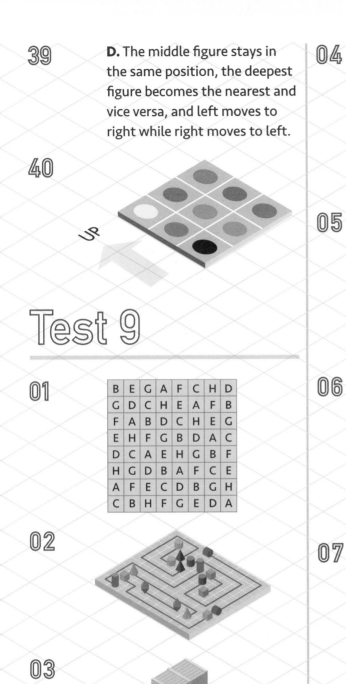

UP

Test 9

01

B	E	G	A	F	C	H	D
G	D	C	H	E	A	F	B
F	A	B	D	C	H	E	G
E	H	F	G	B	D	A	C
D	C	A	E	H	G	B	F
H	G	D	B	A	F	C	E
A	F	E	C	D	B	G	H
C	B	H	F	G	E	D	A

02

03

04

05

06

07

08

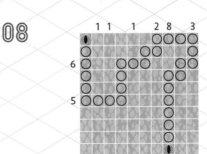

09

1	3	7	9	2	8	5	6	4
8	2	4	6	1	5	3	9	7
9	5	6	3	7	4	2	1	8
4	1	3	5	9	2	7	8	6
5	7	2	8	4	6	9	3	1
6	9	8	1	3	7	4	2	5
7	4	1	2	6	9	8	5	3
2	6	5	4	8	3	1	7	9
3	8	9	7	5	1	6	4	2

10

				1	1	3	3	3	2
				3		2		1	3
		3	2	2		3	2	3	
3	2	1		1	2	1		1	1
1	3		2	1	3	3	2	1	
	2	2	3	2	1	2		0	0
	3		2		3	1	0	0	
	2	1	2		2	2	1		
2	2		2		3				
3	3	3	3	2	3				

11

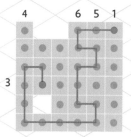

12

clues: top 2; left 3, 3; bottom 3, 5

4	3	2	1	5
2	5	1	3	4
1	4	5	2	3
5	1	3	4	2
3	2	4	5	1

13

Top clues: 32 25 5 9 8 6
Left clues: 1 6 21 17 21 22
Right clues: 14 12 15 21 10 3
Bottom clues: 6 3 13 13 22 23

1	3	7	2	5	4	6
3	7	6	5	1	2	4
7	5	4	6	3	1	2
4	2	5	7	6	3	1
5	4	3	1	2	6	7
2	6	1	3	4	7	5
6	1	2	4	7	5	3

14

0	1	3	3	1	3	5	3
6	6	5	5	1	4	1	4
0	0	4	4	5	6	1	5
2	4	3	0	6	0	2	2
4	2	2	5	6	6	5	6
6	3	0	4	2	0	1	4
0	1	2	5	1	3	2	3

15

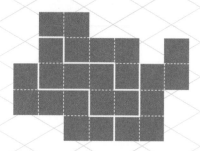

16

1	5	7	8	4	3	6	2
4	2	1	7	8	6	5	3
2	1	3	6	5	8	4	7
6	8	4	3	1	2	7	5
5	3	6	4	7	1	2	8
8	7	5	2	3	4	1	6
7	6	8	1	2	5	3	4
3	4	2	5	6	7	8	1

17

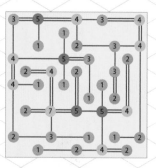

18

55 = 24 + 20 + 11
68 = 25 + 20 + 23
85 = 36 + 40 + 9

19

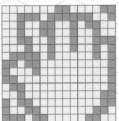

20

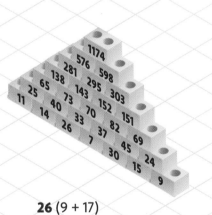

21

22 **26** (9 + 17)

23

24 **84 and 28.** (The age difference is 56, so the grandfather was 56 when the grandchild was born. Halve the age gap and add to the ages to discover the age of the grandfather when he is three times as old as the grandchild.)

25 The monkey is not a farm animal; the goat is not featured in the Chinese horoscope; the rooster is not a mammal. The horse is a mammal that lives on farms and is present in the Chinese horoscope.

26

3	–	1	x	4	= 8
+		+		x	
2	x	8	–	9	= 7
x		–		÷	
5	+	7	÷	6	= 2
= 25		= 2		= 6	

27

1	7	4	2	6	2		7		5	1	0	2
9		9			4	3	6	0		9		9
8	2	0	4		9		3		3	3	1	4
4		4	9	1	3	7	5	3	2	6		5
	3		6		7		2		6		3	
2	6	3	7	2	1	3		2	6	5	4	3
	9		1	4	9	4	7	4	9		8	
3	6	1	5	4		2	4	3	8	7	5	6
	3		3		5		9		4		1	
1		3	2	6	4	9	8	5	7	2		2
3	9	8	6		0		7		1	9	4	3
5		0			2	9	1	5		1		6
8	2	6	0		2		6	5	4	4	3	2

28

2	1	2	1		2	1	4	6
9		2	3	4	5	6		5
3	8	5		1		8	6	4
2	1		2	5	1	3	2	9
	1	2	5	1	8	8	1	
1	9	2	5	7	6		4	7
7	5	1		1		1	1	1
4		3	5	2	9	7		2
2	0	2	9		6	7	0	4

1/25/1881: Edison and Bell form the Oriental Telephone Company.

29 Tom, Paula, yellow gold, bunch of flowers, Lake District, tent. Dick, Fatima, white gold, box of chocolates, Peak District, hostel. Harry, Maria, platinum, coffee pot, Snowdonia, cottage.

30

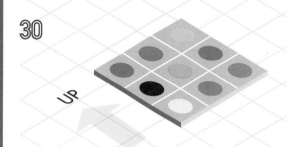

31

32 **60:** (11 – 2) + (211 – 160)

33 **D.** The number of sides of the shapes increases by 3, 4, 5, 6, 7.

34 **520.** The sequence comprises increasing cube numbers, plus the number being cubed: (1 x 1 x 1 + 1), (2 x 2 x 2 + 2), (3 x 3 x 3 + 3) etc.

35 3, 5, 8, 13, 21.

36 12 – 11 + 9 ÷ 5 x 6 = 12
11 – 5 x 6 ÷ 12 + 9 = 12

37 **A.** The smaller shapes move counter-clockwise, with the number of moves indicated by the number of points on the shape.

38 Ten triangles. Triangle = 1, cylinder = 5, hexagon = 6).

39 Bambi, Dumbo, Pinocchio, Peter Pan, Pocahontas, Mulan.

40

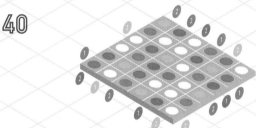

Test 10

01

D	F	G	C	H	E	A	B
C	A	H	E	D	B	F	G
F	B	D	A	G	H	C	E
H	E	C	B	F	D	G	A
B	G	F	H	A	C	E	D
E	D	A	G	B	F	H	C
A	H	E	D	C	G	B	F
G	C	B	F	E	A	D	H

02

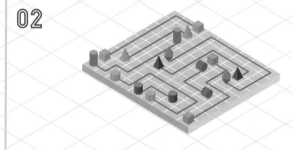

03

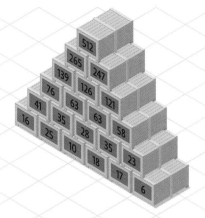

04

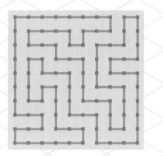

05

06

07

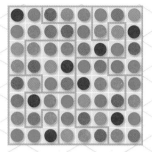

08

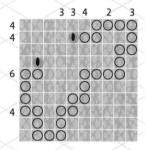

09

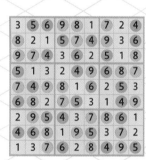

10

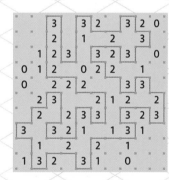

11

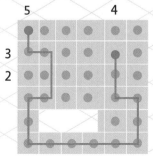

12

```
      1       2
   3  5  1  2  4
   4  2  5  3  1    3
   5  4  3  1  2    4
 3 3  2  1  4  5  3
 4 4  1  3  2  4  5
            2
```

13

```
   26 27 11 12  9  2
   5  6  7  3  1  4  2   33
   6  4  3  1  2  7  5   22
 5 7  3  1  2  6  5  4   13
12 3  2  4  5  7  6  1   15
18 1  5  6  4  3  2  7    7
12 2  1  5  7  4  3  6    3
 6 4  7  2  6  5  1  3   19
19
      4  9  4 19 27 22
```

14

```
2 2 1 4 4 4 2 6
3 4 6 1 0 5 2 0
6 6 3 5 0 3 6 4
2 2 5 0 5 5 6 0
1 1 4 0 3 5 6 4
5 2 5 1 3 1 6 3
1 3 4 2 1 0 3 0
```

15

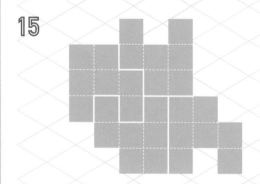

16

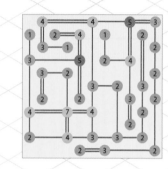

17

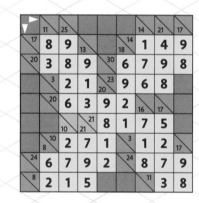

18

57 = 20 + 22 + 15
73 = 28 + 9 + 36
89 = 27 + 22 + 40

19

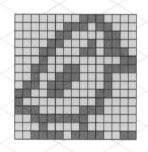

20

21

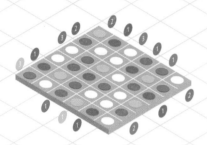

22   **31** (6 + 25)

23

24   **1524:** (102 ÷ 17) x (276 – 22)

25   A great auk is an extinct, flightless water bird; an ostrich is an extant, flightless land bird; a swan is an extant, flying water bird. A penguin is an extant, flightless water bird.

26

9	–	4	x	2	= 10
x		+		+	
5	+	8	–	6	= 7
÷		+		–	
3	x	7	–	1	= 20
= 15		= 19		= 7	

27

2	3	5	1	9	6	7	4	0		3		1
7		4		2		3		4	3	8	4	
3	5	5	6	4	9	0	8	2		2		3
	1		7		3		7		1	3	4	8
5		5			1	2	0	3		7		9
3	9	8	4	1		9		2	8	0	5	6
8		4		4	1	1	3	9		5		0
6	4	1	1	5		7		7	4	3	0	9
2		7		8	7	6	2		8			2
6	5	9	8		8		1		8		4	
0		3		2	3	1	9	8	5	0	5	3
4	2	7	4		1		6		9		0	
4		1		7	0	1	4	2	9	3	4	6

28

11. (**7**, **8**, **12**, **15**, **18**.)

29

30   **C.** The grid rotates 45° counter-clockwise, with the yellow bars alternating between above and below.

31   **5.** The sequence follows the pattern of addition for numbers in odd positions in the sequence, and subtraction for numbers in even positions, starting from 1 and increasing by 1 each time (+ 1, – 2, + 3, – 4, + 5, – 6, etc).

32   Jenny, Snow, Bronagh, September, Monday. Maria, Frost, Deirdre, January, Thursday. Paul, Rainbow, Eamonn, March, Friday. Tommy, Blizzard, Connor, November, Wednesday.

33

20 ÷ 4 x 7 − 14 + 10 = 31
14 − 4 x 10 ÷ 20 + 7 = 12

34

You place six of the boxes on one side of the scale, and six on the other. If the scales balance, none of those twelve boxes contain the extra chocolate – it must be in the six boxes not on the scales. However, if the scales tip, the six boxes on the heavier side must contain the extra chocolate. You repeat the process with the six boxes you have pinpointed, with three on one side and three on the other. Whichever side lowers must contain the box with the extra chocolate. From these final three boxes, place one on one side of the balance, and one on the other. If the balance lowers, the box on that side must contain the extra chocolate. If the balance remains level, the extra chocolate is in the box not on the scales.

35

Nine triangles. (Cube = 1, triangle = 2, hexagon = 3, cylinder = 4)

36

Lleyton Hewitt, Goran Ivanisevic, Richard Krajicek, Andre Agassi, Michael Stich, Pat Cash, Arthur Ashe.

37

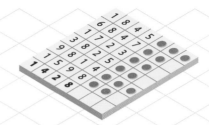

38

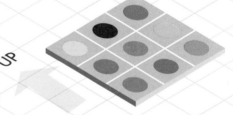

11/18/1928: First appearance of Mickey Mouse, in *Steamboat Willie*.

39

C - Danube. River on which the capital city stands.

40